Robert O. Wood
February 13, 1985

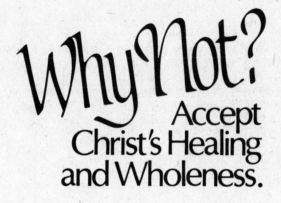

Why Not?
Accept Christ's Healing and Wholeness.

Why Not?
Accept Christ's Healing and Wholeness.

Lloyd John Ogilvie

Fleming H. Revell Company
Old Tappan, New Jersey

Library of Congress Cataloging in Publication Data
Ogilvie, Lloyd John.
  Why not?

  Includes bibliographical references.
  1. Spiritual healing.   2. Jesus Christ—Person and offices.   I. Title.
BT732.5.035   1985   234'.13   83-24871
ISBN 0-8007-1223-4

Contents

TO
Dorothy and Ralph Osborne
for
their love and encouragement through the years
and for
the impact of their lives and ministry
on the church
as a healing community

Introduction
Is Christ Able to Heal Us Today?

We all long to add life to our years and years to our lives.
There is an innate desire in all of us to live fully, now and forever. Yet physical, emotional and spiritual problems debilitate
us and the people we love. We endure disabilities, wondering
how to pray and what we dare expect from our prayers. Is
Christ able to heal us today?

Yes! This book is based on the firm conviction that Christ is
the healing power of the world. What He did to provide healing, wholeness, and health in the bodies, minds, and spirits of
people, during His incarnate ministry, He continues to offer
through His Spirit today. He is the source of healing through
medical science and through the prayers of His people.

How to Pray for Healing

The thrust of this book is how to pray for healing in ourselves and others. We discover the secret of how to do that
from careful observation of how Christ healed people during
His years on earth and in the exciting days of the early church.
From the treasure chest of the many healing miracles of our
Lord before and after the resurrection, we will draw out several
of the most salient to focus on the crucial aspects of His healing
ministry today.

The exposition of these key Bible passages will center our

7

attention on the nature of healing, wholeness, and health; how Christ is performing miracles today; how to pray for ourselves and others; the interrelationship between sickness and sin; the importance of the healing of memories for mental and physical health; how to pray with the full armor of God in confronting Satan's use of sickness to produce doubt and discouragement; how to develop positive attitudes about the Lord's power to heal us; what to do to be open to His grace in the healing of broken relationships; how to get the most out of the periods of life when we suffer, waiting for healing; and how the ultimate healing of our fear of death and dying can happen to us now, so we can live abundantly and eternally.

These crucial themes will be discussed with empathy, so you will identify them with your needs and concerns. The central conviction of each chapter will be illustrated by stories of people today who are experiencing healing and wholeness through Christ and are claiming the power of prayer for a ministry of spiritual healing. The book opens with a personal account of my own long pilgrimage in discovering how to claim and pray for healing.

Healing in Today's Church

There is a growing interest in the church of today concerning healing and healing services. Pastors and church leaders need a sound biblical basis for this exciting development, as well as practical help in avoiding eccentric overemphasis and nonbiblical thinking.

This book grows out of the adventure of my church in claiming Christ's power to heal and the utilization of the gifts of healing He promised to His church. I will share the guidance the Lord has given to me and the elders of the church in developing a healing ministry that is bringing profound renewal to our congregation. Throughout the book, I will explain how to begin, what to avoid, and how to involve the whole church in a healing ministry. We are learning to be authentically biblical in how we pray and what we can expect.

There is a Christ-guided strategy for the church in America today for the healing ministry. It need not emulate the cultural patterns or jargon of groups that emphasize the healing ministry to the exclusion of the whole gospel. Christ called us to preach, teach, and heal. The third must not be left out, but must be done in balance with the first two. The Lord wants to show us ways of being New Testament congregations through which He can care for people's needs, pouring His healing Spirit out for the healing of all facets of life.

Healing: The Many Aspects of Wholeness

When we speak of *healing,* we do not use the word for physical healing alone. In the New Testament, the word *healing* is used to communicate the many aspects of wholeness we desire for all people. The basic Greek word is *sōzō,* the root from which both *save* and *salvation* come. It is also translated as "to make whole." Christ came to save us from our sins, complete our salvation on Calvary, and live with us and in us to make us whole people in every facet of life. He heals us of spiritual estrangement and reconciles us for eternity. We are the chosen, called, and cherished saints of God. But He is not just concerned about our eternal life; He also wants to introduce us to and enable us in the abundant life.

Before salvation, and even after, we acquire mental, emotional, volitional, and physical dis-eases that cripple us in living the abundant life fully. Christ is as concerned about our spiritual, psychological, and physical needs as He is the eternal salvation of our souls. He wants to do for us what He did for the man by the Pool of Bethesda: "... I have made a man every whit whole ..." (John 7:23 KJV). Or as in the New King James, " ... I made a man completely well. ...."

Christ is able to do the same for us. He is the healing power of the world. There is no healing apart from Him. Many in the medical, surgical, and psychological healing professions have learned to cooperate with His Spirit of healing, who is active in the world today. And though sometimes unacknowledged, He is the divine presence guiding the revelation of the discoveries of modern medical research.

The key questions about healing before the church of Jesus Christ today are:

> How can we more effectively cooperate with the Great Physician in the healing of people?
>
> How can we more creatively affirm what the healing professions are doing and pray for them as they work to alleviate pain and suffering?
>
> At the same time, how can we claim our rebirthright as the community of prayer, acknowledging that Christ sometimes heals directly as a result of prayer and always seeks to answer prayers for the strength, courage, and hope of those who suffer mentally or physically?

Whenever a church or an individual takes seriously Christ's commission to pray for the sick, there are three troublesome concerns that tend to confuse. One is that not everyone gets healed in the way or in the timing we've prayed for. This tends to create reticence to pray boldly. Another is the concern over false expectations. We are tempted to hold out the promise that the Lord will deal with everyone in the same way. We deny His immense originality in how He works with His people and promise that everyone will be healed in the same way. The third problem is that we put the focus on our prayers and not the power of the Lord. That prompts some to claim to be healers and pile up the statistics of successes. America has several examples of "faith healers," especially in television, who employ bizarre and eccentric methods that draw attention to the human agent rather than the Great Physician.

These three concerns keep many Christians and most congregations from prayers for the healing of all the needs of people. That's a tragedy, since the risen Christ is as powerful to heal today as when He was incarnate as Jesus of Nazareth. He entrusts the gift of healing to His church and to individuals who are willing to pray for the manifold needs of people, leaving the results to Him and taking no glory for themselves.

People long to be whole. There are unconfessed sins, haunting memories, broken relationships, compulsive patterns, fears, and distorted thinking that debilitate that wholeness. Many get sick or are unable to regain strength because of mental attitudes, and sometimes they lack hope or even the will to live. We must seek to be therapeutic congregations, speaking to the real needs of people and creating an atmosphere in which they can receive prayer and healing for their needs. Just as Jesus ministered to the whole of human personality to impart the gift of wholeness spiritually, psychologically, and physically, so must we do in our preaching, teaching, counseling, and prayer. That requires a clear understanding of what the Bible says about wholeness and how the beloved community, the Body of Christ, is to communicate it.

This book is tailored to grapple with what healing by the Great Physician is all about and to encourage Christians to move forward as congregations, daring to be healing communities. We need to confront the simplistic heresies that distort biblical teaching: such as the idea that lack of healing is caused by an inadequate faith or unconfessed sin hidden in the sufferer; or if our prayers don't work, that there is something wrong with the one who prayed. Our task is to help bring people and their spiritual, psychological, physical, interpersonal, and circumstantial problems to the Great Physician. They need sound biblical counsel about how to seek His healing and how to be expectant of the many ways Christ answers.

My plan for this book is to remain true to my calling as a biblical expositor. I am neither a trained medical authority nor an accredited psychologist. The insights and truths from the healing arts will be utilized to exemplify the basic thrust of the passage being explained rather than to imply any "almighty" statements. My task will be to communicate the love and power of the Great Physician and to learn from the healing miracles how He can and will continue His ministry in people today. Each of the Bible passages examined will lead us into an aspect of the healing ministry of the Lord.

I want to express my profound gratitude to my administrative assistant, Jerlyn Gonzalez, for her encouragement throughout the writing of this book. Her typing of the manuscript through several revisions, at a time in her life when she was discovering anew the healing power of the Great Physician for her own physical recovery of wholeness, added reality and inspiration for the project.

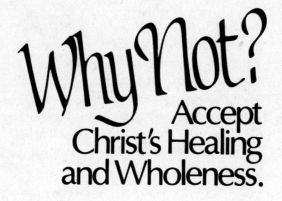

Why Not? Accept Christ's Healing and Wholeness.

1 Why Not?

One snowy winter morning in 1955, when I was a student at the University of Edinburgh, Scotland, I awoke with a stirring sense of excitement. I had an inner feeling that it was going to be one of the most important days of my life.

As I dressed in heavy underwear, warm sweaters, and tweeds, in preparation for a long day in chilly, damp classrooms, the feeling of anticipation mounted. I tried to discern the cause of the surging hopefulness. Was it because I sensed that I would finally find an answer to the searching questions I had been asking?

During my time of study, completing my education for the ministry, I had confronted my own deep spiritual need. Even though I had been a Christian for several years, I lacked spiritual power. I fully accepted that Christ had died for my sins, and that through the power of the resurrection, I would live forever. The concern was how to live the abundant life now. Inside I was much the same person I had been when I became a Christian. I was insecure, anxious, and uncertain.

My orthodoxy provided me with a firm belief in the inspired authority of the Scripture. Therefore I believed without question the account in the gospels of the mighty works and miracles of Christ during His ministry as Jesus of Nazareth. I accepted the record of His continued ministry through the apostles in the Book of Acts and in the first-century birth and growth of the church. My questions, however, were about the extent of the availability of Christ's power in the twentieth century. What could we boldly pray for and expect in living today?

Pinned to a Mat of Theories

At that point, my orthodoxy had me pinned to a mat of theories that immobilized me. I was hammerlocked with the idea that the effluence of the Spirit displayed on the pages of the Book of Acts had been limited to that period for the establishment and expansion of the church. The gifts of the Spirit, such as wisdom, knowledge, faith, healing, and working of miracles, I thought, were not for today. Christ's promise, ". . . Lo, I am with you always, even to the end of the age" (Matthew 28:20), was taken to mean to the end of the apostolic age. Occupied with what Christ had done for me in the cross and resurrection, I had no personal relationship with Him as a present Lord. Meanwhile I was left to live out His way, truth, and life on my own obedience and faithfulness. I was losing the wrestling match with questions about how to do that. As I struggled, the countdown of the referee had begun. I was pinned and about to lose not only the match, but also the will to keep on wrestling to find the answer.

Yet I couldn't give up. The promises of Christ haunted me. The more I studied them, the more convinced I was that I was missing something—Someone! What Christ had said on the night before He was crucified, alarmed me. "Most assuredly, I say to you, he who believes in Me, the works that I do he will do also; and greater works than these he will do, because I go to My Father" (John 14:12). Then He promised that He would return after His crucifixion, resurrection, and ascension. He promised a Helper, the Spirit of truth, and power. And then He defined who that would be:

> I will not leave you orphans; I will come to you. A little while longer and the world will see Me no more, but you will see Me. Because I live, you will live also. At that day you will know that I am in My Father, and you in Me, *and I in you.* He who has My commandments and keeps them, it is he who loves Me. And he who loves Me will be loved by My Father, and I will love him and *manifest Myself* to him.
>
> John 14:18–21, *italics added*

My burning question was whether this promise was meant for just the apostles and the first-century church or was for all time until the Second Coming, when history as we know it would end. My losing battle to live the Christian life on my own strength was convincing me that Christ's words had to be for now as much as for the first-century Christians.

I longed for the reality of what Christ had also promised would be given in His indwelling presence: "Abide in Me, and I in you . . ." (John 15:4). As I studied Christ's warning that His followers could do nothing unless they abided in Him and He in them, I readily agreed with His caution. I knew He was right: I had tried on my own, and it wasn't working.

Breakthrough: My Unpinning

All these turbulent, probing questions were invaded that morning in Edinburgh with an undeniable assurance that a breakthrough was about to happen. The sense of excitement mounted all through breakfast and during my long walk to the Mound, just above Princes Street, where New College, the theological school of the university, is located. Little did I know that my class that day with Dr. James S. Stewart, my beloved professor of New Testament literature and theology, would be the hour of my unpinning from the mat of my constricting ideas about the contemporary ministry of the risen Christ.

It happened near the end of Dr. Stewart's lecture on the present, indwelling power of Christ. He was speaking about the very passages in John's gospel with which I had been wrestling. He spoke of Christ as our living contemporary and our lives as His postresurrection home. With a fine blend of biblical scholarship and contemporary illustrations, Dr. Stewart vividly described what it meant to abide in Christ and for Him to abide in us. Truth I had heard before suddenly struck fire in my mind, sending a bolt of lightning through my entire being.

Then just before Professor Stewart ended his lecture, he paused, whipped off his glasses, as was his custom in moments of intense inspiration, and stood looking out the window as if transfigured by a vision of Christ Himself. Then in crisp, penetrating words so characteristic of his teaching and preaching, he said, "If we could but show the world that being committed to Christ is no tame, humdrum, sheltered monotony—but the most exciting adventure the human spirit can know—those who have been standing outside the church and looking askance at Christ will come crowding in to pay allegiance, and we may well expect the greatest revival since Pentecost." Stewart concluded his lecture with his firm convictions of Christ's indwelling, transforming power in us today. I was stirred profoundly and decided then and there that I wanted to be part of that revival. "Why not?" the question throbbed in my heart.

Throughout the rest of the day, I thought of little else. Christ was alive! More than a historical figure locked on the pages of the New Testament or aloof in heaven, He was my living contemporary. His promises were true—not just for the first century, but for my life in the last half of the twentieth century.

At the end of the day I knew I could be a part of that renaissance Dr. Stewart had talked about. But I also realized that nothing could happen through me that had not happened to me. The day concluded on my knees. I committed all that I had and was or would ever attempt to be and do, to the Lord. I felt His presence that night and felt the invasion of His presence and power pulsate through my mind, emotions, will, and body.

My remaining time in Edinburgh was filled with new adventure as I finished my studies. I longed to get on with an active ministry of sharing the secret I had experienced.

Soon the busy, demanding life of a pastor put me in touch with the immense needs of people. I discovered they not only needed a clear teaching and preaching of eternal life, but also an introduction to the power of the indwelling Christ to live the abundant life. I found Christians everywhere in the very same condition I had experienced. They longed to be whole, to know Christ's healing in their lives. Mental, emotional, and physical problems debilitated them. As I visited the sick, counseled the disturbed, and worked to mend strained and broken relationships, I was forced to grapple with further questions about how to communicate Christ's healing power for our lives today.

What Healing Can We Expect Today?

Is Christ able and willing to do in our lives today what He did in the lives of people during His ministry as Jesus of Nazareth? Can the same miracles He did through the apostles be expected and prayed for today?

These questions pressed me into an in-depth, prolonged study of Christ's healing and the ministry of healing entrusted to the church. My investigation into the mysterious nature of spiritual, emotional, and physical healing occupied my mind during the first seventeen years of my ministry. It led me to a profound respect for the surgeons, physicians, and psychiatrists with whom I worked in the front-line trenches of human suffering. They, too, longed to understand the causes and cures of human sickness and were open to a close working relationship with me in efforts to combine the use of their skills with my prayers for their patients. They saw that their task was to remove obstructions to healing and provide needed medicines to aid in healing, but realized that healing, when it took place, was a mysterious miracle.

As the years went by I pored over the Scriptures and devoured every piece of literature I could find about the power of prayer in the healing process. That led me to begin to pray specifically in Jesus' name for the healing of the manifold needs of individuals. Amazing things happened. People got well sooner than expected by their doctors. The assurance of the intervening touch of the Master on their lives provided a positive mental attitude and maximized the healing process. Some who had been declared hopeless by medical science recovered.

Claiming that Christ's healing was available today for all facets of physical, mental, and relational problems, I found an amazing openness among the lay elders of my church to hold healing services, at which time the needs of people could be surrendered to the Lord, leaving the results to His timing, plan, and purpose for people. Again Christ released His power and pressed me on in a growing discovery of His desire to use both medical science and the prayers of the church in the ministry of making people whole.

Allow me to share the basic understanding and convictions that grew in me during this period. My pilgrimage begun that day in Edinburgh quickened. As the years went by I became more bold in claiming the power of Christ in prayers for healing. All that I want to expand on in subsequent chapters of this book is based on the progressive step-by-step formulation of my thinking that brought me to an answer that posed the most daring question of all.

Christ: The Healing Power of the World

Basic to all else, I was gripped by the essential belief that Christ is the healing power of the world. He is the creating, re-creating heart of God, Immanuel, God with us in the world. As the eternal Word of God, the Logos, He created the universe, hung the stars, and initiated all levels of life on our planet earth.

John 1:1–3 became the foundation stone of my thinking. "In the beginning was the Word, and the Word was with God, and the Word was God. He was in the beginning with God. All things were made through Him, and without Him nothing was made that was made." Now note that John goes on to say that the same Word who created us came to begin a new creation. "And the Word became flesh and dwelt among us, and we beheld His glory, the glory as of the only begotten of the Father, full of grace and truth" (John 1:14). He came to reveal the heart of God and to embody the wholeness He had intended for humankind in the beginning.

Paul sounds the same triumphant note:

> He is the image of the invisible God, the firstborn over all creation. For by Him all things were created that are in heaven and that are on earth, visible and invisible, whether thrones or dominions or principalities or powers. All things were created through Him and for Him. And He is before all things, and in Him all things consist.
>
> Colossians 1:15–17

One of the key words of the New Testament used to describe Christ is the Greek word *archēgos,* translated as "author" or "prince." The word clarifies who Christ is and what He came to do. It means "one who takes the lead and provides the first cause; the authority, the source and originating instigation." The One through whom we were made came to remake us. That awesome fact is crucial for our understanding of what Christ did as Jesus of Nazareth.

He came to make us whole again. We were created to know and love God. We were given the gift of freedom to choose to glorify Him and serve Him. Humankind's misuse of that freedom fractured the wholeness God intended. The sad tale of history charts the result. Our "no!" to a dependent, trusting relationship with God became the inherent tendency in human nature. It is called sin—the desire to take charge of what only God can control and the refusal to take control of what He has placed in our charge. Sin is missing God's mark, seeking to run our own lives, trying to be our own gods.

The result was a disharmony, instead of the sublime harmony God had planned for us. Inside us the perfect unity intended between the thinking brain, the limbic system that controls our emotional responses, the autonomic nervous system, and the body's function was affected. Distorted thought triggered confused emotions and malfunctioning of our body systems. Our endowed immune system was debilitated. Meanwhile the harmony intended between us and the natural world was fractured. Out of fellowship with God and filled with the tension of running our own lives, we were at enmity with nature. At the same time hostility, envy, and competition replaced the love and mutual caring we were meant to express to our fellow human beings.

All creation had fallen from its grand design because of our rebellion. Suffering, disease, germs, and crippling sickness became our lot. And in the vacuum of the separation from our Creator, a mysterious, hostile force of evil became rampant in the world.

Yet the Lord did not give up on us. Out of this fallen creation He called a people—Israel—to be His people and entrusted to them the Ten Commandments, the rules and regulations of healthy living in the midst of the world. The Lord guided and cared for His people, and the checkered history of Israel's mixture of response and resistance to the Lord is the stirring and startling story of the Old Testament.

Then, at the lowest ebb of history, the Author of Life, the Logos—Christ Himself—came to begin a new creation, reconcile us to God, and call a new Israel, the church. The One through whom God had created and sustained life came to redeem life in all dimensions.

A clear understanding of who Christ is helps us understand what He did to make men and women whole during His ministry in Palestine. He ministered to people as persons, caring for their minds, emotions, and bodies, as well as their souls. As God's creating and recreating heart, He was healing incarnate. When Christ touched the sick, deranged, or troubled, they were healed. The blind received sight, the lame walked, and the mentally disturbed were liberated.

Just as Christ made the bold claim to be the Light of the World, Truth Incarnate, and the Life, so too He was the focused power of healing. The recreative power to bring soundness of mind, to return body systems to normalcy, and to heal tissues and cells—which had existed in Him with God—was now channeled in mighty force through Him in His message, touch, and His exorcising authority. Our understanding of His miracles begins there, or it has no beginning at all.

Healing: Understanding the Word

The next step in my growing understanding of healing was to do an in-depth review of the word *healing* in the New Testament. There are three words that are used particularly to describe what Jesus did. The word *sōzō* is used for "salvation" and "healing." The noun form is *sōtēria,* meaning "deliverance from danger, suffering, sin, and sickness." This word is used to describe the eternal salvation for which Christ lived, died, and rose from the dead. Jesus described His essential healing ministry in John 3:17: "For God did not send His Son into the world to condemn the world, but that the world through Him might be saved." Here the word *sōzō* is used. He came to liberate us from the bondage of sin, sickness, death, and to make us whole again. As divine Savior (*Sōtēr*) He called men and women to eternal life forever and abundant life now.

A second word for healing is *iaomai,* variously translated as "to heal" and "to make whole." It is used twenty-two times in the New Testament to describe physical healing. The healing of the daughter of the Canaanite woman is an example of this: ". . . And her daughter was healed from that very hour" (Matthew 15:28). The word is also used of spiritual healing, as in Christ's words quoting from Isaiah 61:1 to declare His purpose: "He has sent Me to *heal* the brokenhearted" (Luke 4:18). James, in his epistle, uses *iaomai* for the healing of both physical and spiritual needs (James 5:13–16).

The third word used in connection with healing is *hugiēs*. In the gospels it describes the state of being well or whole. This is the word used in Jesus' question to the man by the Pool of Bethesda: ". . . Do you want to be made well?" (John 5:6). The King James renders it, "Wilt thou be made whole?" The same word is employed to describe what happened in Jesus' healing of the man with a withered hand: "Then He said to the man, 'Stretch out your hand.' And he stretched it out, and it was restored as whole as the other" (Matthew 12:13).

All three of these words, and a few others used less frequently, are descriptive of Jesus' healing ministry in the lives of people. He cared for individuals, seeking to set them free of sin and sickness. As the *archēgos,* the Author of Life, He could not do less. But He did so much more. He went to the cross to atone for our sin and to take on Himself our suffering and sickness.

Healing at the Foot of the Cross

So the next natural step in my pilgrimage in search for understanding and an experience of Christ's healing led me to the foot of the cross. What actually happened there? I knew that the discovery of power for a healing ministry was inseparably related to what happened on Calvary. Two things captured my

attention: what had been prophesied about the Messiah's atoning death and what Jesus said about it Himself before the cos-
mic event.

In search for clarity, I focused on Isaiah 53, carefully study-
ing the Hebrew words describing what the prophet foresaw
would be accomplished by the Messiah for our healing and re-
demption. Note verses 4 and 5 particularly:

> Surely He has borne our griefs
> And carried our sorrows;
> Yet we esteemed Him stricken,
> Smitten by God, and afflicted.
> But He was wounded for our
>   transgressions,
> He was bruised for our iniquities;
> The chastisement for our peace was
>   upon Him,
> And by His stripes we are healed.

I became very excited as I considered the fourfold healing
predicted by Isaiah. The Messiah would bear our griefs, carry
away our sorrows, be wounded for our transgressions, and
be bruised for our iniquities. When I probed the meaning of
the words, I was particularly startled by the words *borne,*
carried, and *sorrows.* The word *nasa,* "has borne," means "to
lift up," "bear away," or "remove to a distance." It is the
word used in Leviticus 16:22 to describe the action of the scapegoat.

The idea in ancient Israel was that the sins of the people
were placed on a goat and then the goat was led out into the
wilderness. This gave the people an assurance that the Lord
had removed their sins. The instruction of the Lord to Moses

for Aaron was "The goat shall bear [*nasa*] on itself all their iniquities to an uninhabited land; and he shall release the goat in the wilderness" (Leviticus 16:22).

In a much more profound way, Jesus Christ was our scapegoat. The sins of the whole world were placed on Him for Him to carry away on Calvary in His suffering and death. The word "carried," from *sabal* in Hebrew, denoted assuming a heavy burden, as used by Isaiah here. It means an actual substitution.

But what did Christ carry away for us? The Hebrew word *choli,* translated in its plural form as "griefs," actually means "sickness" or "disease." The word *makob,* translated in the plural as "sorrows," means "pain."[1] Isaiah's prophecy really means that in the substitutionary sacrifice of the Messiah He would bear and carry away sickness as well as our transgressions and iniquities. The peace that He established for us carried the full meaning of the Hebrew *shalom,* "wholeness, salvation, a right relationship with God, and a soundness of mind, spirit, and body."

Matthew's commentary on the Isaiah 53:4 prophecy guides our understanding of how Jesus perceived the prediction about Him. Surely Jesus talked about that, and then years after the ministry of healing and cross of the Master, Matthew wrote this word of explanation of Christ's mighty works. ". . . And He cast out the spirits with a word, and healed all who were sick, that it might be fulfilled which was spoken by Isaiah the prophet, saying: 'He Himself took our infirmities and bore our sicknesses' " (Matthew 8:16, 17).

On the cross Jesus did battle with the debilitating powers of sickness, sin, and death. And those who accept the Lord's liberating and atoning cross and receive Him as Savior become the recipients not only of the status of forgiven sinners, but also of the wholeness He makes possible.

Preach, Teach, and Heal

The pulse beat of my pilgrimage quickened. When Christ rose from the dead, He commissioned His disciples to go into the world and do three crucial things: preach, teach, *and* heal. All power in heaven and earth would be theirs. The promise that His followers would do what He did and greater things was to come true!

The "greater things" meant both quality and quantity. No longer confined to the incarnate ministry after His resurrection, ascension and return in the power of His Spirit, the Lord was ubiquitous and omnipresent, continuing what He began as Jesus of Nazareth. And the greater works in quality was that the disciples were able to introduce people to Christ as victorious Lord; Savior, through the atonement of the cross; and indwelling power, able to enter into the minds, bodies, and souls of those who believed in Him.

I considered with delight and amazement the way Luke opens the Book of Acts. "The former account I made, O Theophilus, of all that Jesus began both to do and teach" (Acts 1:1). The key word is "began." The incarnation was the beginning of Jesus' ministry of the new creation. Luke describes the dramatic account in Acts of how that ministry was continued. At Pentecost, the Lord filled His followers with His Spirit. Then the wondrous miracle happened. In His name, calling on the power of His name, the apostles preached salvation, led people to Christ, and healed the manifold spiritual and physical needs of people. The Lord was faithful to His promise to abide in them and release His power through them. A few hours after Pentecost the disciples knew Christ better than they had as a result of following Him for three years.

As I read Acts 3, the account of the healing of the lame man at the gate of the temple, I realized that Christ's indwelling

Spirit had produced the gifts of faith, healing, and the working of miracles. When Peter and John met the lame man, saw his impotence, and remembered Jesus' promise to heal through them, it must have been a challenging moment of risk and daring. I imagine that they felt a stirring within them. What would Jesus have done? He would have healed the man. Could they, dare they? It was then that Christ abiding in them released the gift of faith to believe they could. When Peter took ahold of the man's hand, the miracle began to happen. He lifted the man and spoke the name of Jesus: "In the name of Jesus Christ of Nazareth, rise up and walk" (Acts 3:6). Then divine, healing energy flowed into the sockets of the man's ankles. A joining together, an articulation, took place, linking what had been out of place. Now the gift of faith was released in the man, and by the power of the living Christ, he walked, leaped, and praised God. It had happened! Christ was healing through the apostles.

As I pressed on in investigating the healing of Christ in the early church, my mind was held in rapt attention. Each healing was done with the effluence of daring faith that it could be done and then the bold declaration of the name of Jesus Christ. As I considered this amazing period of Christian history, I began to wonder why we had become so timid in claiming Christ's power to heal in our time.

Careful study of the subsequent centuries immediately after the apostolic age charts a demise of spiritual healing. I am convinced that the cause was not that the Lord was reluctant to continue the gifts of daring faith, healings, and working of miracles. Rather, the demise resulted from lack of the quality of openness to the living Christ exemplified by the apostles. For example, the rite of anointing with oil for healing of the manifold sicknesses and needs of people in the third century became the rite of extreme unction, reserved for the dying. The service was performed by the priest in assurance of eternal life, not as a means to enable healing for living the abundant life.

Coupled with the lack of emphasis on spiritual healing was the growth of the practice of medicine. Though it was part of the ministry of the church in the early centuries, the practice of praying for the healing of persons lessened. Often, in periods of spiritual revival, renewed experience of the gifts of the Spirit broke forth, and faith healing was revitalized.

The Reformation was mainly concerned about the primacy of justification by faith, rather than by indulgences and works. Luther made a point of stressing that the gifts of the Spirit were reserved for the apostolic age, but later in his life both preached about healing and prayed for healing miracles.

The reformer's emphasis on faith, however, began a new freedom in Christendom. The Reformation was a watershed return to the inspired authority of the Scriptures and to faith as the only basis of a right relationship with God. The reverberations of that rumbled through the sixteenth to the eighteenth centuries, producing new movements of people who claimed the power of the risen Christ. Eighteenth- and nineteenth-century revivals followed naturally. The result in the last half of the nineteenth century and the first half of the twentieth century were two distinct emphases. One was the growth of Pentecostalism, with an emphasis on the baptism of the Holy Spirit, the experience of the gifts of the Spirit, the Spirit-filled life, and a ministry of faith healing. At the same time Mary Baker Eddy founded Christian Science on the firm belief that evil, sin, and sickness did not exist and that total freedom from physical disorder and disability was attainable through Christ-conditioned thinking.

But most hopeful of all in the twentieth century has been the rediscovery of the healing ministry by the traditional churches. It has been distinguished by an affirmation of the church's role in the healing of persons. In the main, it has been coupled with an affirmation of medical science as one of the ways Christ, the healing power of the world, is at work today. But in addition to that, pastors, church officers, and denominations have sought ways of claiming Christ's power to heal through prayer. It is this mainline renewal of the church that has become a focus of my life and ministry.

Now let me recap what were the basic discoveries of this pilgrimage in my own life, which I've tried to describe:

1. Christ is the healing power of the world. There is no healing apart from Him. He seeks to make people whole today as He did during His ministry as Jesus of Nazareth and as resurrected Lord in the first century.

2. Christ seeks to make His church a healing community—founding, fostering, and supporting the work of medical science and claiming His healing through prayer. The healing resulting from both comes from Him alone.

3. Contemporary Christians in whom He abides have an inalienable right to claim and exercise the spiritual gifts of faith, healing, and working of miracles today.

4. The task of the local church is to preach and teach wholeness and to help its people to claim healing through prayer, providing services of healing in which prayers for the needs and problems of people can be prayed with the confidence and assurance of Christ's intervention in keeping with His greater wisdom and His evolving strategy in our lives.

My seventeen-year pilgrimage had brought me to a place of clarity and confidence. It also developed a realization that I could not lead a congregation as a healing community, seeking wholeness for its people, without the consistent abiding power of the indwelling Christ in my life. That brought me to my knees again, seeking what I have called in other writings, "the other half of the blessing."

My passion was not only to abide in Christ as a recipient of His atoning death and eternal security, but also as a recipient of His abiding in me. The same prayer I'd prayed that night in 1955 in Edinburgh, Scotland, was renewed. The years in the ministry—preaching, teaching, and caring profoundly for the needs of people—had been exhausting and draining, and they had brought me to a new sense of my own inadequacy. Again I felt the need to become a riverbed for the flow of supernatural power from the indwelling Christ. I was broken open again and realized a new infilling of His power.

2 Why Not, Indeed?

When I began my ministry in Hollywood, now twelve years ago, I inherited a group of elders who were wide open to being guided into the adventure of leading a congregation that was a healing community.

I will never forget the first evidence of the outpouring of Christ's healing power. At a retreat with the elders—early in my ministry at Hollywood Presbyterian Church—I outlined four inventory questions to guide our thinking together.

- What kind of people are we called to deploy into the world?
- What kind of church sets free that kind of people?
- What kind of elders enable that kind of church?
- What kind of pastoral leadership inspires that kind of elders?

We defined our goals and searched for answers to the questions. The kind of people we were to deploy into the world were people whom Christ was making whole. They would be people whose experience of Christ had healed them in their basic relationships: with Him, through grace; with themselves, through Christ's esteem and acceptance; with others, through unqualified affirmation by His power; and with the world, through a willingness to become involved in the needs and problems of individuals and in specific areas of society to alleviate suffering and injustice.

We focused a vivid picture in our minds of the quality of our members' ministry in the world. Boldly we claimed the biblical calling of all members to be in ministry. We reaffirmed that anyone in Christ was in the ministry, and the gifts of the Spirit were for that ministry.

We solidified our purpose: to place in the world people who were committed to Christ as Lord and Savior; who were filled with His Spirit; who could share their faith with others; and who would seek to live under the implications of Christ's kingdom, His reign and rule in all of life.

That pressed us to clarify the quadrilateral calling of our church life and purposes. We dedicated ourselves to move forward as:

1. A worshipping congregation
2. A healing community
3. An equipping center
4. A deployment agency for evangelism and mission.

The Church: A Healing Community

The task of the church as a healing community forced me to call on the resources of my seventeen-year pilgrimage. During that retreat I poured out all that I had learned and experienced. As a result the elders rose to a fresh commitment to develop the life of the Hollywood Presbyterian Church as a community of believers in which people could receive wholeness through Christ's healing power.

At the conclusion of our study of healing, I was very aware that one of the elders, Dr. Robert Hicks, a psychologist and educator, was looking at me intently. He was wearing a rubber neck brace and obviously was in great pain because of an injury. Then another elder spoke up. "Pastor," he said, "we've been talking about healing, and Dr. Hicks has been sitting here in pain. Why don't we gather around him and claim the healing power of Christ for which, as elders, we've been called to pray?" A serendipity was upon us. The room was electric with Christ's presence and power. We laid hands on the good doctor and claimed healing in Christ's timing and way.

The following Sunday Bob Hicks was sitting in the front pew of the sanctuary of the Hollywood church, with the neck brace off and free of pain. The ministry of prayer healing had begun. That Sunday Bob handed me an anonymous poem that became the theme of the new song that pulsed through our hearts.

> Filled with a strange new hope they came,
> The blind, the leper, the sick, the lame.
> Frail of body and spent of soul . . .
> As many as touched Him were made whole.
>
> On every tongue was the Healer's name,
> Through all the country they spread His fame.
> But doubt clung tight to his wooden crutch
> Saying, "We must not expect too much."

Down through the ages a promise came,
Healing for sorrow and sin and shame,
Help for the helpless and sight for the blind,
Healing for body and soul and mind.

The Christ we follow is still the same,
With blessings that all who will may claim.
But how often we miss Love's healing touch
By thinking, "We must not expect too much."

Over the years, we have continued praying for the spiritual, psychological, relational, social, and physical needs of people.

In that first year we held the first healing service one Sunday evening. In preparation we studied James 5 about the calling of the elders to pray for the sick, ministering with prayer and the laying on of hands. Hundreds of people came forward to submit their needs to Christ through the prayers of the elders. This practice has continued in services at various times, on retreats for the members, and in the many small groups that meet throughout the community for Bible study, sharing of needs, and prayers for each other.

A Time of Trial and Testing

During this period of my spiritual and intellectual growth in understanding the healing ministry of the Great Physician in the Hollywood Church, I faced a personal time of trial and testing concerning what I was preaching and teaching about Christ's healing power. As I have explained in other books and messages, my wife, Mary Jane, was stricken with cancer and underwent five major surgeries.

The temptation during those dark days was to question what I had discovered on bright, shiny days of inspiration. Yet through it all, we both were drawn closer to the Lord and to each other. Instead of contradicting our emphasis on healing, her illness brought a clear note of reality and authenticity to Christ's presence and power.

When people would ask, "How could this happen to your wife with all you say about Christ's healing power?" my only response would be: "That's not the issue—what's important is to claim the Bible's teachings and promises for a person who needs Christ's healing in an urgent way right now. Don't raise doubting questions—pray!"

Often Mary Jane and I experienced low times when our own prayers were inadequate. At one point, Mary Jane found it difficult to pray at all. Then a friend reminded her, and me, that those were the times we had to depend on the prayers of faithful friends. And that's exactly what we did. Thousands of people in our congregation and all over the nation prayed for her healing. And at several of the healing services, Mary Jane went forward for prayers of healing by the elders. One of those times marked a dramatic remission and the beginning of healing and strength. As is often the case, the dawn breaks after the darkest hour of the night.

Three things account for Mary Jane's healing. She's a fighter and doesn't give up. The Lord honored that and kept alive her belief that she would get well. Second, she was surrounded by the positive influence of love from people near and far. By a wondrous *Christotelepathy*—Christ-filled spiritual communication between people who love and pray—she was lifted up and encouraged. Then by utilizing the treatment and medical care and by the implanting of His own Spirit in malignant cells, Christ healed over the prolonged period of recovery. The result was that the pilgrimage in spiritual healing Mary Jane and I have shared through the years was not interrupted or negated, but profoundly deepened.

The Pilgrimage: A New Step

A recent stage of that pilgrimage has also been very exciting and revealing. Two years ago, the elders of our worship department met to discuss a paper I'd written for them on worship. The purpose was to reaffirm the biblical guidelines of worship and set new goals for caring about what concerns our people. At the end of the paper, I listed several questions. One of them was, "How can we minister to the manifold needs of our members and visitors in the Sunday-morning worship, caring for individuals and responding to specific spiritual, emotional, and physical problems?" The question arose out of the realization that people who came to worship were moved by the singing and preaching of the Word and had no opportunity to make a personal response either to accept Him as Lord and Savior or to receive help with particular hurts and hopes touched by the service.

The elders took ahold of that question like a hungry brown bass taking an enticing bait. They wouldn't let it go for two hours of intense discussion. The upshot was a new plan to conclude each morning service with a time of laying on of hands by the elders. A plan was devised to give an invitation after the sermon, calling people to come forward for prayer during the closing hymn of dedication.

In preparation for their ministry, the elders were again trained in how to pray, bringing particular needs to the Savior's healing power. The results on the first Sunday we tried the plan were so gratifying, the session (the ruling board of elders) voted to make prayers for healing at the conclusion of each Sunday-morning worship a permanent part of the order of worship. Now, on a rotating basis, six elders at each service take their places in the chancel and are available to pray with individuals who respond to the invitation.

As with most churches, what is presented in Sunday-morning worship affects the thinking and life of the church as a whole. Services of healing can be scheduled at various times in the week without drawing much attention. To make a healing ministry a part of Sunday-morning worship is mainlining that emphasis into the lifeblood of the Body of Christ, the church.

Added to the blessing received by thousands of people during the past two years through this healing ministry, by far one of the greatest boosts to the church is what has happened in the lives of the elders themselves. They have the fresh exhilaration of seeing Christ work His contemporary miracles. No one, pastor or elder, is elevated as a healer. The gift of faith and healing is given for the needs of people, not for personal aggrandizement. The power of the Lord is released week by week, and the glory goes to Him.

All this is in cooperation with, not in exclusion of, the ministry of healing of medical science. Medical advice is not given by the elders, pastors, or the growing number of people in the congregation who are claiming the calling to pray for others. Our task is to put people in touch with the Master and to affirm the many ways He heals today.

What I've tried to do in the opening chapters of this book is to describe the guidance the Lord has given me though the years about His available power to heal the needs of His people. As I intimated, these long years have brought me to an answer that now raises a bold question: Why not?

There are questions we ask in search of an answer, and then there are questions prompted by the answer. This is true for any researcher who asks probing questions until he or she finds an answer and then asks the question of implication and application, "If this is true, then what?" So my question in response to the undeniable evidence that Christ is healing is: "Why not experience His wholeness, healing, and health today?"

Ever since Calvary, the resurrection, the effluence of His Spirit in the first century, and His healing power in any generation that would take the time to discover the secret of how He works in us, the question has not been what He will do, but *what we are willing to allow Him to do through faithful prayer and surrender of our needs.* Our task is to carefully observe the Great Physician in the New Testament, first as Jesus of Nazareth, as our liberator on the cross, and then as the instigator and implementer of healing in the early church. As we get inside the skins of the people He touched with healing, we will learn how to claim and pray for His healing in ourselves and others today.

As we do that I ask you to become part of an adventuresome "why not?" fellowship. That question is the theme of my life. So often I ask it at the end of messages. And when I'm confronted by a difficult problem and Christ guides me to an answer, I must ask it again for myself. The first time I asked it was that day in Dr. Stewart's class. I've never stopped asking it since. Why not, indeed?

> The quest was searching and restless
>   Persistent, demanding, and hard
> The answer was very exciting
>   A truth we cannot disregard
> The years of questioning are over
>   The night of doubt is done
> Now is the dawn of the answer
>   Abundant life has begun
> The answer raised a bold question
>   Our hearts with fire burn hot,
> The Great Physician is with us,
>   And so we ask, "Why not?"

3 The Gift and the Giver

Recently I was in Naples, Florida, on a preaching mission. One afternoon, after speaking in the morning, I returned to my hotel room to rest and prepare for my evening message. I didn't anticipate that the Lord had a very special gift in store for me that would give me an exhilarating rejuvenation far more renewing than the nap and time of study I had planned.

As I walked into my room, the phone was ringing. "Hello! This is Peggy Lickel," the pleasant voice said. "Remember me?" Before I had a chance to assure her that I did, she recounted the very unusual and tragic circumstances of our meeting. She reminded me of the double funeral I had conducted one day in Los Angeles for her mother-in-law and a brother-in-law. Both had died a few hours apart. Peggy's other brother-in-law, Henry Lickel, who lives in the Hollywood area,

had called me to help the remaining family through the difficult time of the loss of two loved ones.

The funeral service was one of those moving times when the
Lord intervenes with comfort and strength. He gave the an-
guished family hope and courage in their grief. I felt His power
surging through the Scriptures I read and the thoughts He
guided me to share. A liberating peace and joy in the assurance
of Christ's victory over death pervaded. He was present to heal
the hurting hearts with the conviction that death is but a transition in the midst of eternal life for those who belong to Him.
Peggy, the family, and friends left the chapel with a touch of
heaven upon their souls. That was the last time I had seen her.

She and her husband returned to Sanibel Island, Florida,
soon after the funeral. Several months later she was diagnosed
as having a very serious kidney disease. One day she was
rushed to the emergency section of a hospital in Fort Myers,
where her condition was diagnosed as serious, and her prognosis was proclaimed to be less than hopeful.

In the quiet loneliness of her private room, Peggy reflected
on what was happening to her and she longed to recover the
peace she had experienced in Christ's presence that day at the
funeral. In a moment of mixed anguish and longing for
Christ's presence and power, she raised her hands in a plea and
cried out, "Lord, help me!" When she dropped her hands, one
of them fell on the remote control of the television set in her
room and pressed the ON button. To her utter amazement, she
had clicked on our church's television program, "Let God
Love You."

It was the last five minutes of the program, but just as the
picture and the sound came into focus, I was quoting Christ's
words, "Lo, I am with you always" and "I will never leave you
or forsake you." Peggy said she could hardly believe it. The
same words I'd said at the funeral, which had given her peace

then, were repeated as if just for her in her new hour of need.

Peggy went on to say the significant thing was that she was released of fear. She felt Christ's presence with her there in her hospital room. He gave her the gift of freedom from tension over the outcome of her sickness. Whether or not she got well became secondary to the fact that she had experienced an immediate answer to prayer. She was assured that Christ knew about her need for Him. Anything else was unimportant. What she had needed was the Great Physician Himself. Whatever He gave her in addition to His loving, uplifting presence was simply a plus.

Now months later, continuing to grow in strength and health, Peggy's voice on the phone was strong and lilted with Christ-inspired joy. She had wanted to come to my preaching mission in Naples. When that didn't work out, she just had to call. She made my afternoon, my week, my month. I thanked her for ministering to me by telling me what had happened. Now as I write about it months later, the delight of it all lingers.

Peggy's story is a dramatic account, but not unusual. Whenever people cry out, "Lord, help me!" He hears and responds. In fact, I'm convinced that He initiates the desire and responds to the prayer He's instigated.

What Is It for You?

What is it in your life and mine right now that makes us want to cry out for help from the Great Physician? Physical pain, a lingering sickness, a frustrating problem, a strained or broken relationship, some memory that lingers with haunting fierceness, stress that jangles nerves, worries that won't go away? We all need the Master's touch. What is it for you?

Focus on whatever is your need, whatever keeps you from wholeness of mind, body, or spirit. With that specific need in mind, our consideration of one of Jesus' most significant miracles of healing will become intensely personal. The account of the healing of the paralyzed man by the Pool of Bethesda in John 5 is power packed with insight into the Great Physician Himself and the how and why of His healing ministry—then and now. Let's look at what happened, Jesus' explanation of why it happened, and then consider how it can happen today.

Picture the scene at the Pool of Bethesda in Jerusalem. Multitudes of sick people were gathered on the five porticos around the pool. The name *Bethesda* means "house of mercy or loving-kindness." And that's exactly what the lame, blind, and diseased people hoped it would be for them. The belief was that at divinely appointed times of mercy, an angel would descend and stir up the pool. The first person into the pool after the stirring of the water, it was believed, would be healed.

When Jesus came to Jerusalem for the feast, He was drawn to this gathering place of human need. I picture Him standing off to the side, surveying for a long time the mass of human suffering. Sense the anguish of His loving heart as He looked into each face. Watch the look of sorrow in His eyes. That's how He looks at you and me when life prompts us to call out for help, sometimes in longing for healing too deep for words.

One man among the infirm there at the pool particularly caught Jesus' attention. The man had been there for thirty-eight years. Imagine it! He was carried to the pool on many of his 13,870 days of crippled impotence. That's a long time to wait for healing.

But pause for a moment to reflect on why John selected this incident out of the treasure chest of his memory of Jesus' healings and made a specific point of the thirty-eight years. I have often conjectured that perhaps the reason he gave so much attention to this account of what happened at the pool was be-

cause he saw the similarity between the thirty-eight years of
this man's paralysis and the thirty-eight years Israel wandered
in the wilderness after the first aborted attempt to enter the
Promised Land of Canaan. A careful study of the dating of
that first attempt in Numbers 10:11 and a consideration of the
amount of time that had elapsed from the beginning of the ex-
odus from Egypt and the period spent at Mount Sinai reveals it
was about two years. That means the subsequent wandering in
the wilderness was thirty-eight years, not forty, as often stated.

You remember what happened to the people of Israel. Even
though God had extricated them from Egypt, had appeared at
the Red Sea, had given them the sign of His presence in the
pillar of cloud by day and of fire by night, and had revealed
His plan and purpose in the Ten Commandments on Sinai, the
people were afraid to go into Canaan and possess the land.

The glowing reconnaissance reports of Joshua and Caleb
about the land flowing with milk and honey were rejected, and
the hostile enemy forces of Anak filled them with panic. They
turned away from the propitious moment the Lord had ar-
ranged and wandered to and fro in the wilderness for thirty-
eight years.

Maps indicate that the wilderness area was comparatively
small. That suggests that the people moved back and forth for
a long period because of their fear and unwillingness to claim
what God had promised. They could not claim what was
theirs!

This puts John's emphasis on the length of the paralyzed
man's waiting at the pool into a very interesting light. Perhaps
he was suggesting that the man's will to be well had been
dulled by the long time and that now he neither expected nor
anticipated a miracle for himself. A long period of suffering
does that to us. When our prayers are not answered when we

expect or in the way we've told the Lord we want Him to act, we become impatient and then hopeless.

Do You Want to Be Made Whole?

This perspective on the paralyzed man's situation helps us to understand Jesus' question to the man. "Do you want to be made well?" The King James renders the question, "Wilt thou be made whole?" Did Jesus discern that perhaps the man had given up? Had he become so accustomed to being ill that he could no longer envision himself as well? The years of being a cripple had debilitated the desire to be whole.

The same thing can happen to us in our prolonged physical disabilities, personal problems, or relationships with difficult people in our lives. Perhaps we become accustomed to hurting circumstances around us, thinking they can never change. And what about the solidification of our attitudes into personality patterns that we no longer want to change?

Jesus' question, "Wilt thou be made whole?" blows the cap off our reservations on our own grim prognosis of the possibility of life being different for us. Do we really desire healing? Intense desire for the Master's help in any area of our lives is a vital, necessary prerequisite for receiving His healing.

The man by the pool had a carefully rehearsed set of excuses. He blurted them out as if he had said them so often they were spoken with little thought. Other people were to blame for his not being healed. When the propitious stirring of the water occurred, no one would help him get into the pool, or when he was helped, some other of the infirm got in before he did. For thirty-eight years? We wonder about that!

Instead of saying, "Yes, I desire to be made whole," the man accused others for his plight. First he felt helpless, then hopeless, and finally resentful. That resentment rendered him incapable of responding to the great moment of opportunity presented to him. And the man's attitude probably made him the kind of hostile, negative person others least wanted to help. I think that's also part of what attracted Jesus to him. The Master has a way of picking out those on whom others have given up.

That touches a raw nerve in us. Blaming others for our problems multiplies the difficulties. Someone, something, must take the rap. Often our prayers, if we say them at all in our low moments, are filled with complaints rather than a humble confession of our need. Our resentments over people and life can block the flow of Christ's Spirit into us and the areas of need in our minds, emotions, and bodies. That blockage must be broken open by the Master before He can penetrate to our deeper problems. The good news is that He persists with us in spite of the picket line filled with complaints erected around our hearts.

In the case of the man by the pool, Jesus broke the picket line and swept all his excuses aside. He commanded him to ". . . rise, take up your bed and walk." This admonition tells us so much about how the Lord seeks to enable wholeness in us. First, He had to change the man's picture of himself. Rise? Walk? That's the one thing he could not do. He thought of himself as an invalid, not as one who could lift himself, much less walk. The Lord pressed the man to the edge of his perceived impossibility. He focused his attention on the one thing he thought he could never do again. Jesus knew the man had to get a new image of himself before His healing power could help him.

What Wholeness Do You Need?

Again, back to us. What would it be for you right now? What new picture of wholeness do you need from the Master to pray for with boldness? Often we need to pray for guidance about what to pray, how to make supplication for our needs. When we take time to meditate, asking the Lord for His guidance on what to ask for, He leads us to the very things we cannot do in our own strength.

Many of us pray only for what we could accomplish with our own abilities. The Lord wants to lead us out into an adventure of trusting Him for His enabling power for what only He can do for us and through us. It may be the tackling of some awesome task or the daring to show initiative in expressing love and forgiveness or the willingness to trust Him with a problem for which there seems to be no solution. Then it may be a physical illness or disability that has persisted in spite of the finest medical care. At the very time we are ready to give in to the idea that things will probably never change, the Great Physician asks us to trust Him completely.

Now notice a further implication of the command of Jesus to the man by the Pool of Bethesda. The Master's challenge to "rise, take up your bed and walk" also expressed a need for a break with the past. Why else did Jesus ask the man to take up his bed? Wasn't walking miracle enough? No, Jesus did not want him to make a provision for a relapse. The man might have been tempted to leave that tattered old bed in its place, just in case, after a few hours, he had a relapse. The man had taken a long time to get his place in the queue leading up to the water. He might not have wanted to give up his place in line!

We can appreciate what might have been the main caution. It's difficult to cut off our dependence on worry, fear, and complaining. Trusting Christ and not our methods of compensating for our condition is scary at times. Problems and difficulties can become more acceptable than the unknown, the untested.

Courage to Trust the Great Physician

Only a personal encounter and abiding relationship with the Great Physician Himself can give us the courage to trust Him with our problems. So often we think we have to conjure up enough faith to qualify for His healing of our manifold needs. We falsely suppose that if our lives are all in order and we word our prayers perfectly and trust Him completely, He will then pay attention to us.

The man by the pool had nothing but his need. And it was in the majestic presence of the Master that he could dare to do what He commanded. It was the dynamic healing power of God focused in the Lord that liberated him to dare to walk.

I've often tried to picture the look on Jesus' face as He gave the man the stirring command to rise and walk. I think His eyes communicated hope and strength mingled with deep compassion and empathy. His whole being radiated tender caring. But surely there was also an unmistakable authority that must have made the man trust His admonition. Magnetism and majesty resounded in His voice.

I am convinced that it was when the man looked into Jesus' face, felt the full impact of His divine power, and sensed the rebirth of new hope leaping up inside his own soul, that he said, "I can do it! Why not?" When the Master's desire for him and his desire for himself were one, the miracle of healing took place. The man leaped up and stood and then walked for the first time in thirty-eight years. Imagine these first steps: Caution at first and then as his confidence grew he walked around in sheer delight over the wondrous thing that had happened to him.

The secret was too good to keep. The man walked through Jerusalem, his bed in hand, telling everyone he met that he was

healed. The scribes and Pharisees were among those who observed the undeniable evidence of his healing and heard his
exclamation of joy. And they observed something else with
disdain and consternation. The man was carrying his bed on
the Sabbath. That was absolutely forbidden by the multiplicity
of regulations about what was classified as work. The man was
breaking the Sabbath rules!

It is difficult for us to imagine that the stringent religionists
saw only infractions of the Sabbath rules and could not rejoice
over an obvious miracle. All that concerned them was that
someone had healed this man on the Sabbath, and the man
was carrying his bed. The leaders wanted to know who was
behind this. "Who told you to take up your bed and walk?"
they demanded. We are both alarmed and amazed that the
man didn't know who it was who had done this wondrous
healing in his body.

A Further and Deeper Healing

The Master was also concerned about this. That's why He
sought out the man for a further and deeper healing. We learn
from that another secret about how the Master seeks to make
us whole today. When He found the man, He did three crucial
things for him.

First, the Lord confirmed a new self-image for the man. He
affirmed him as a healed person. No longer should he think of
himself as a debilitated paralytic. "See, you have been made
well . . . ," He said with encouraging enthusiasm. The Lord entered into the man's delight, sharing the blessing of healing. He
was thankful that power for healing had flowed through His
touch, and He rejoiced with the man's exuberance.

Second, the Master was concerned for the man's total wholeness. He knew that the healing of his physical disability was

only a beginning in the experience of complete wholeness He desired for the man. With profound sensitivity to his deeper needs, Jesus said to the man, "Sin no more, lest a worse thing come upon you."

Does this mean that the Lord identified some sin that had caused the thirty-eight years of disability he had suffered? Perhaps. Yet there's something even more significant than that in the Lord's words. As the Messiah, sent into the world to confront and heal the root problem of humankind's estrangement from God, He could discern that the healing of this man's body was only the beginning of the wholeness He had authority to impart and enable. More than just the healing of his legs, the Lord knew the man needed a healing of his total nature. His mind needed to be reoriented to be an expression of this response of praise and obedience.

Note carefully that prior to this second encounter, the man not only didn't know who it was who had healed him, but he did not praise God for the gift of healing he had received. That is indicative of the nature of his sin before and after his healing. He had endured suffering without seeking God and had neglected to praise Him after he was liberated from it.

We get a picture of a person who was enduring his vicissitude without a vital quest for God's help. That is revealed in his response when Jesus asked him if he wanted to be made well. If God had been the source of his hope for healing, surely he would have explained that as the reason he came so consistently to the Pool of Bethesda. Rather, as we have seen, he complained about people's lack of caring for him. The extent of his faith was in the magic of the stirred-up water in the pool. If his dominant desire had been a longing for God's Spirit for his needs, wouldn't he have witnessed to that when Jesus confronted him with the penetrating question about whether he really wanted to be made well?

The Wholeness Jesus Wants to Give

The wholeness Jesus wanted for the man was what He called all people to so urgently: a complete trust in God, a personal relationship with Him, a willingness to receive His love and forgiveness. The opposite of that is sin as we defined it in the first chapter—missing the mark, separation from fellowship with God, and the anxious endurance of life's struggle in our own strength. All other sins come from that root. From the basic sin of separation from God, Jesus warned that the man would be vulnerable to a "worse thing." He would miss knowing God's love now and would spend eternity in the same estranged and separated condition. A worse thing, indeed!

John does not record in detail the conversation with Jesus and the man. However, he subsequently records Jesus' analysis of what happened to that man not only by the Pool of Bethesda but in this second encounter with Him. In John 7:23 Jesus clarifies that He "made a man completely well." The King James renders it, "I have made a man every whit whole." The Greek means, "I made a whole man, whole." That indicates more than the healing of his body. Complete spiritual, emotional, volitional, as well as physical healing had been accomplished in what must have been a profoundly personal conversation. The Lord was concerned about every facet of the man's nature and the interrelationship of his thinking about himself and God and about his future physical and spiritual health.

That's one conversation, referred to so briefly by John, to which I wish I had been a silent listener and an unnoticed observer. Yet from the more completely recorded conversations of Jesus, such as with Nicodemus or the Samaritan woman at the well, we can be assured that He led this man into a realization of his deeper needs and of Jesus' unlimited love, flowing from the heart of the Father, through Him, for the whole man.

The wonder of it all is that the Lord continues to seek that kind of communion with each of us today. He begins with whatever need we have and then moves into all the areas of our lives. He seeks to make the whole of us to be whole. He honors our plea for help in our physical, spiritual, emotional, or relational needs for healing. Then He uses that as a beachhead to claim the whole territory of our character and personality. And He does it with the authority entrusted to Him as Immanuel, God with us.

I'm thankful that the man Jesus made whole returned to the Pharisees to tell them who it was who had healed him. His witness about his Healer was no longer a generality. Now he told them forthrightly that it was Jesus who had healed him. That led to an open conflict between the Jewish leaders and the Master. Good thing. In that dispute Jesus boldly declared the secret of His healing power. What He said becomes the bedrock foundation of our understanding of the healing power available to us through the same Christ today. What He was and did then He continues to be and do in our lives today.

The Healer: God Himself

What enraged the Jews in Jesus' explanation of His ministry is the vital source of our enlightenment and encouragement. He uncompromisingly asserted His equality with God in His ministry, power, and authority. "My Father has been working until now, and I have been working" (John 5:17). The cooperation between the Father and the Son in creation and providential care expressed since the beginning of time was now continuing through the ministry of the incarnate Son on earth. That's why the man had been healed.

Then Jesus went on to declare that all His mighty works
were under the guidance and direction of His Father:

> Most assuredly, I say to you, the Son can do nothing
> of Himself, but what He sees the Father do; for what-
> ever He does, the Son also does in like manner. For the
> Father loves the Son, and shows Him all things that He
> Himself does; and He will show Him greater works
> than these, that you may marvel. For as the Father
> raises the dead and gives life to them, even so the Son
> gives life to whom He will.
>
> John 5:19–21

In so stating, Jesus claimed that the Father, who is the Source
of all life, had entrusted to Him the power to impute new life.
All His works and miracles were to this end.

Later, in John 10:10, Jesus made the same awesome declaration: ". . . I have come that they may have life, and that they
may have it more abundantly." He revealed life as it had been
intended to be lived, went to the cross to defeat the enemies of
life manifested in sin and death, and rose from the dead to assure us that ". . . because I live, you will live also" (John 14:19).

The continuing ministry of Christ with us is to add life to our
years and years to our lives in this phase of our eternal life and
then, at the point of our physical death, to raise up our inner
spiritual selves to an endless existence in heaven. He is profoundly concerned about helping us live at full potential in this
life and forever. That's His assignment by the Father. What He
seeks to do in your life and mine to make us whole is backed
up by all power in heaven and earth. In Christ, the healing
heart of God and all our hurts meet.

All this is summed up in Jesus' further statement that day in

His disputation with the Jews, "Most assuredly, I say to you, he who hears My word and believes in Him who sent Me has everlasting life, and shall not come into judgment, but has passed from death into life" (John 5:24). Christ is not just the only way to God; He is God's only way to man.

Belief in Christ today frees us of four distressing things we never have to do again:

1. We don't have to question our worth to the Lord. He came and comes in search of us. Long before we called out for Him, He was at work in us creating our desire to know Him and receive His love, forgiveness, and healing.

2. We don't have to justify ourselves. He has made us right with Himself on Calvary. The power to believe that and trust Him is His gift.

3. As His beloved and cherished people, we don't have to question that He cares. He is with us and will help us as we surrender all our needs to Him.

4. We don't have to worry about the future. Jehovah-Shammah, "The Lord is there," will go before us to prepare the way. The Lord lives in us. From within He will release healing power for our bodies, wisdom for our minds, the fruit of His Spirit for our emotions, and resiliency for our challenges and difficulties.

Claim Your Gift, Possess Your Possessions

Our only responsibility is to claim what is ours already. The petulant tendency of self-justifying religion is to put off to some future time what Christ offers now. I like the way Obadiah and Paul sound the admonition to possess our possessions and accept all that is ours. The two men lived over eight hundred years apart but communicated the same urgent encouragement. Obadiah prophesied the Messianic promise, and Paul reflected on the glory offered us through it. Both drive home the point I've been seeking to make in this chapter.

Obadiah declares that there will come a day when the people of God will realize all that the Lord has done for them. "But on Mount Zion there shall be deliverance, and there shall be holiness; the house of Jacob shall possess their possessions. The house of Jacob shall be a fire . . ." (Obadiah 17, 18). Note the two things the Lord does and the one thing we will be freed to do in response. The deliverance prophesied we understand from this side of Calvary. We have been delivered from the power of evil and sin. Holiness results. That means belonging to the Lord and growth in His likeness. That process is realizing the wholeness that is offered for every aspect of our lives.

And what is our part in the miracle? Simply to possess our possessions. Two Hebrew words are used for possessions in different manuscripts. One is *môrāshêhem*, "what is ours by right," and *môrîshêhem,* "our dispossessors." Both have exciting implications when interpreted in the light of our deliverance through Christ's life, death, resurrection, and abiding, indwelling presence with us. He is our Lord and Healer. And through Him we can claim overcoming strength and courage in our battle with the dispossessor of sickness and the difficulties of life.

Christ is greater than the force of evil in the world. By His name we can claim Christ's victory. We don't have to struggle alone. And the secret of that is possessing our possessions—Christ, His healing power, the gift of faith to trust Him completely, and His moment-by-moment release of hope.

Now look at Paul's reflection on all that is ours because we belong to Christ. ". . . For all things are yours . . . the world or life or death, or things present or things to come—all are yours.

And you are Christ's, and Christ is God's" (1 Corinthians 3:21–23). Nothing is left out. The same love of the Father that was given to the Son is now focused on us and is poured out on us through Him. And knowing that, we can live our years in the world, facing all that happens in the present or the future without fear.

Victorious Living Now and Forever

Couple Paul's assurance that all things are ours with Jude's conviction of Christ's present help, and you have a formula for victorious living in life's difficulties:

> Now to Him who is able to keep you from stumbling,
> And to present you faultless
> Before the presence of His glory with exceeding joy,
> To God our Savior,
> Who alone is wise,
> Be glory and majesty,
> Dominion and power,
> Both now and forever. . . .
>
> Jude 24, 25

Don't miss the "now and forever" dimensions of that doxology.

Christ comes to us to keep us from stumbling into discouragement and doubt in times of physical and spiritual need. Because of His atoning death, we are presented as faultless, totally exonerated, declared not guilty. Through His presence with us we are no longer helpless or hopeless. And the wholeness He is enabling in us now will be complete when He walks with us through the valley of the shadow of death and introduces us into the rejoicing company of heaven.

I'm constantly amazed at how little most of us expect and settle for in the living of our faith. We live as spiritual paupers even though we are heirs of a magnificent inheritance. But then in times of distress we are brought to the end of our meager resources and finally begin to draw on what is ours already.

A friend of mine in Texas told me the story of a Texas family who refused to possess their possessions. They lived at a near poverty level on a small piece of dry, parched land. It was difficult to eke out a living on the ranch that had been handed down to them. One day a representative of an oil company offered them a large sum of money for the property. Tests had proven that there was a good possibility of oil under their land. The father of the family refused the offer. "Our family has been living on this land for generations. There's not been oil in the past, and there won't be in the future!" he said defiantly. He and the family continued to live their meager existence until he died; then the children were free to sell the land and claim what had been theirs all along. Too often we are like that man in not claiming our spiritual blessings of wholeness.

The Lord asks us what He asked the man by the Pool of Bethesda, "Do you want to be made whole?" When we respond with a resounding, "Yes, Lord, now and for eternity!" He is faithful. Whatever our need, He takes us at our word of willingness. He takes our surrender seriously. He heals us spiritually with love and forgiveness. He changes our attitudes about our helplessness and releases His healing Spirit in our bodies. Our great need, above all needs, is for a relationship with the Great Physician Himself.

One Sunday morning Morris and Sue Faulkner, a middle-aged couple in Ventura, California, traveled the over fifty miles to our church in Hollywood. They had been to our services before. He had attended one of our Sunday services a few weeks earlier with a friend from out of town, and so had suggested to his wife she might enjoy attending.

The Lord spoke to them through not only what was said in the service, but the love they felt from the people. During the period when we turn and greet one another, they had been warmly welcomed. The invitation at the conclusion of the service for the people to come forward for prayer with the elders was the most moving part of the worship experience for them. They felt a profound stirring inside of them as they watched other people come to the chancel for prayer.

As usual, the invitation had been inclusive for people to receive Christ as Savior, surrender their problems and perplexities, seek guidance for the next week, and express openness for Christ's healing in physical and spiritual needs. Both the man and his wife felt the need to commit their lives to Christ and come to know Him as the Great Physician over all their concerns. Yet neither of them overcame his or her reticence to come forward.

On the journey home to Ventura, they both shared what they had felt when the invitation was given. They rejoiced over the impact of the service in their lives and affirmed the fact there was an opportunity for personal caring.

The next Sunday, they felt impelled to return, this time with his visually handicapped daughter. They wondered if she too would be touched by the power of God they had previously felt. Again at the conclusion, the same invitation was given. This time the husband and wife encouraged each other, and to their amazement when they got to their feet to make their way forward, the daughter said, "I want to go, too." Soon all three were making their way toward one of the elders. It happened to be Fred Grayston, a staunch supporter of the healing min-

istry from the very beginning. Here is Fred's own account of
what happened.

At the conclusion of the eleven o'clock service, I was
sitting on the side aisle, near the front of the sanctuary.

You gave the invitation, including in your remarks
the invitation for persons to come forward to accept
Christ.

There were quite a number who came forward to
pray with the elders. Although I was not assigned that
morning, I sensed there were several who were waiting
their turn, so I went forward to help and immediately a
family came to me.

There were three—apparently father, mother and
daughter. They were from Ventura, had listened often
to our television program "Let God Love You," and
had come down to our service before, including the
previous Sunday, when you had also given the invitation to come forward. I asked them if they wished to
accept Christ as Savior and Lord. Each responded
tearfully in the affirmative as they hugged each other,
and I embraced them and we all prayed.

They told me that on the way home the previous
Sunday they had talked about the wonderful feeling of
worship and friendliness and the challenge they had
heard to make a commitment to fill the void in their
lives. They said to each other that they would return
and if the invitation were given again, they would respond.

So, on this Sunday, when the invitation was given
they nudged each other and said, "Let's go!" And they
did—not only the husband and wife, but also his
daughter.

I heard each of them confess their newfound faith, and I prayed with them for some time. Seldom have I seen such a happy, thrilled, and tearful family. The man said as he dried his smiling face, "We've finally done it!"

Lloyd, the important factor here, in addition to the working of the Holy Spirit in their lives, was the invitation. I am certain that every Sunday, God is dealing with someone who is ready to take this step of faith. And we must never neglect to provide the opportunity.

The man and wife, and their daughter, Susan, have since been baptized and have become members of our church. We are thankful that the man's company moved its headquarters to Thousand Oaks from Ventura, thus bringing them forty minutes closer to Hollywood and an active participation in the church.

Our pastor of caring and counseling, Ralph Osborne, took an interest in this family who were going out of their way to attend and join our church and inquired how it was that they were first drawn to our church. The man wrote Ralph Osborne this letter. I want to share its contents because it exemplifies the wonderful way the Giver draws people to Himself to impart His gifts.

Dear Ralph,

Thank you for your letter of welcome to my wife, my daughter, and me. You asked me what brought us to your church, so here's how it happened.

Ted Hope of Lookout Mountain, Tennessee, is an old friend I had for some reason always kept somewhat at arm's length, even though our friendship had stood the test of time, as well as an even tougher trial; we had at different times in our business careers each worked for the other. I admire and respect Ted for his business talents, but there is more than Ted's good education and natural ability that sets him apart from others. It seems, in addition to his vitality, he has an inner glow not characterized by many people in the business world.

One day last year Ted flew into Los Angeles on business. He telephoned me from his hotel, inviting my wife and me to meet him for Sunday brunch in Hollywood some miles from our home in Ventura. I readily accepted. My wife suggested she stay home and catch up on things she had to do. I told him it would be great to see him again. Then he said "I've got a better idea. Why don't you go to church with me and then we will go eat and catch up on old times." I laughed nervously and said, "Ted, you don't need me to help find your way to church. I think you know I don't go to church. I'm an agnostic and haven't been in a church in years."

With a lilt only Ted's voice carries, he said, "Well, that's all right, but I think you would enjoy it. I know the pastor, and I'd like you to meet each other." I stuttered something about my presence threatening the durability of the church's structure, but he enthusiastically persisted. I looked at the surprise in my wife's eyes as I said, "Okay, Ted, if that will make you happy, I'll go to church with you. What time should I meet you, and where is it?"

Sunday at 9:15 A.M. I was standing on the sidewalk in front of the First Presbyterian Church on Gower Street in Hollywood, waiting for my friend's arrival—wondering what I was doing there and why I had agreed to go with him.

Suddenly he appeared, radiant and smiling. We exchanged greetings and went inside. Shortly the service began, and I started to feel an emotion well up in me as the choir sang and the organ played and you and Lloyd, and your associates began pouring out the wonderful story of Jesus and His love. I strained hard to control myself, promising God if He would let me out of the place without making a public spectacle of myself, I would return. He did, and my friend and I went on to spend an enjoyable lunch and visit.

I never let on what had happened to me, I wasn't sure myself, but I'll never forget the probing look in Lloyd's eyes as I was introduced to him at the foot of the stairs, following the service.

I left the church knowing Jesus is God. I couldn't have made it through the service without Him. Yes, I kept my promise—I returned and have many times since. My wife and I have accepted Jesus Christ as our personal Savior and we are now fledgling Christians trying hard to do His will.

So many wonderful blessings have been bestowed on us since giving our hearts to Christ it would be difficult to tell you all of them here; especially in regard to my daughter. We have recently learned God has an unlimited variety of ways to heal. In her case He has greatly improved her vision through the use of specially designed contact lenses, which in turn has improved her ability to learn, has calmed her, and quieted her frustrations and as a result has made it possible for her to enter an adult program designed to prepare her for independent living.

We give all the glory for these wonderful happenings and much, much more to Jesus, since we have become

witnesses to His power and His love, all before we were
baptized and taken into the church. Imagine what can
occur in our lives as we continue to be filled with His
Spirit.

We also thank God for wonderful friends like Ted
Hope of Tennessee, who are willing to reach out to
those who are lost in the darkness of this world without
Christ. I would encourage more Christians to be like
Ted Hope.

This man's story, reflected from these various perspectives,
reaffirmed my conviction that the gift and Christ the Giver are
inseparable.

So in the next chapter we will turn out attention to how to
get in touch with the Lord Himself. Only then can we claim
what He has done for us and offers to do in us. When we give
up the assumption that we should tell Him what to do, what
He does is usually far greater than what we expected.

>   You are coming to a King
>   Large petitions to Him bring.
>   For His grace and power are such
>   That you cannot ask too much!
>   JOHN NEWTON

4 How to Pray for Yourself When You Need Healing

Do you ever talk to yourself? Of course, we all do. It's a kind of thinking. Inside all of us there is a continuous dialogue going on with ourselves. In that deeply personal exchange, we sort out what's happening to us, mull over how we feel, and rehearse what we are going to say or do in challenges or opportunities ahead of us.

Sometimes, when we think we won't be overheard, our dialogue becomes audible. That can be very embarrassing if someone listens in on us. It used to be said that it was a sign of old age when we started talking aloud to ourselves.

The other morning, I was carrying on a conversation with myself while I was dressing. I was thinking through an important conference that I was to have later in the morning. What would the people involved say? How were they going to react?

One of my responses I actually spoke aloud. "Oh, really?" I

said with mingled concern and consternation. My wife overheard my audible question. "What did you say?" she asked.
Red faced I replied, "Sorry, dear, I was talking to myself." She
laughed and said, "Forgive me for interrupting. Carry on, but
please turn down the volume. I thought you were talking to
me!"

In search of secure places where they can talk to themselves,
some people enjoy the privacy of their automobiles while driving alone. Ever notice a person driving a car next to or behind
you, who is talking avidly and then realize that there's no one
else in the car?

Recently while creeping along in the slow lane of the freeway, I looked into my rearview mirror and observed the man
in the car behind me in heated dialogue with himself. He
looked very angry as he carried on his one-way conversation. I
imagined what he was saying and suspected his consternation
was punctuated with four-letter words. When he noticed me
watching him in the mirror, he smiled sheepishly and threw up
his hands in a helpless gesture that communicated, *Well, who
doesn't talk to himself?* and then, *Why don't you mind your own
business?* He seemed relieved when my destination prompted
me to turn off at an exit. I imagined he said to himself, *What's
this world coming to? I can't even talk to myself in my car on the
freeway without being interrupted!*

Actually, a constant flow of dialogue takes place inside us
while we are talking to other people. We talk over in the private chamber of our minds what we think the other person is
saying, what's really meant beneath the words, or how we are
going to respond once he or she stops talking. Sometimes we
actually say within ourselves what we are going to say or what
we'd really like to say if we dared.

Have you ever wondered what it would be like to have a
mechanical device attached to your ear, which could transmit

people's inner dialogue with themselves into audible sounds, so that you could know what they were saying to themselves? It might help us to get to the point more quickly. So seldom do we say what we are really thinking.

I've often reflected on what it would be like to preach to people with an audio transmission of their real thoughts being translated immediately to me as I spoke. It would give me instantaneous feedback: some points belabored too long, others unclear, raw nerves touched that need tender sympathy, responsive chords in souls plucked that bring the listener and me into oneness.

Inner Dialogue: Real Thoughts and Feelings

One thing is certain. Often our inner dialogue reflects more of what we are really thinking and feeling than what we say— and what's more important, what we pray. True prayer is when we take the deepest longings of our conversation with ourselves and articulate them into our supplications and intercessions. The tragedy is that we talk honestly to ourselves, then often we speak to our Lord in a studied, pious way. Sometimes we leave out of our prayers the most urgent needs we should bring to Him. Our conversation with ourselves has determined what is proper and plausible. All too often, we've decided that what we need to ask is impossible. Our deepest concerns, which we talk over with ourselves, often do not get into contact with the Lord.

That's especially true in our conversation with ourselves before we say our prayers for the healing of our own needs— physically, emotionally, spiritually, interpersonally. We ask and answer negatively for ourselves questions that tumble about in our minds. Questions like these: *Is Christ able to heal me as He healed people during His earthly ministry? Does He know or care about my pain, my turbulent emotions, my hurting memories, my broken relationships? How can He care about individuals, with the millions who are in need of healing? How can I, one person, make contact with the Master?*

Ever asked and answered those questions with doubt? Who hasn't? And have you found that by the time your inner dialogue with your uncertain self was finished, you had little faith left to pray with any boldness or assurance?

I don't have a miraculous transmitter attached to my soul to hear your answers, but from thirty years of ministry, listening intently to people's needs, I can hear you saying, *Yes, all too often I'm my own worst enemy when it comes to praying for healing for myself. I have faith in Christ to save my soul for eternity, but I'm really unsure of how to appropriate His healing power for my needs.*

Quite honestly, I've wondered about people who say He's healed them and really doubt the stories about faith healing some people tout so glibly. Then there are the questions about people who have prayed and not gotten well. Add to that the array of suffering all around me in the world, and I find that by the time I get around to praying about my needs, all I dare to ask for is the strength and courage to endure. Sometimes, I even wonder if the Lord hears that prayer. There are so many talking to Him at the same time, how can He focus attention on my needs, much less release His healing for me?

Sound familiar? Ever talk to yourself that way?

Changing Doubt to Daring Prayer

Would you like to have your inner dialogue of doubt transferred to daring prayer? You can!

What happened to a woman in the crowd around Jesus at Capernaum one day, can happen to us. She pressed through the crowd and touched the tassel on Jesus' robe and was healed of a bleeding, cancerous sore on her body. For twelve years she had suffered the oozing, infected, painful malady. Yet when she touched the Master, she immediately felt healing surge through her body.

But a greater miracle took place before she touched Him. It was the transformation of her inner dialogue from fearful exasperation to faithful expectancy. A careful reflection on the account of this woman's healing helps us to discover the power of impelling faith that frees us from our doubts and gives us boldness to place our real needs before the Master.

Some background is helpful. Reading the story of the woman's healing in Matthew 9:20–22; Mark 5:25–34; and Luke 8:41–48, we can piece together the broader picture of two miracles—one in her own dialogue with herself, in her thinking, and the other in her daring touch of the Master that resulted in her physical healing.

We are told that the woman had suffered twelve years, had been to many doctors, and had depleted all her money, seeking a cure. Reading between the lines, with a knowledge of the Levitical regulations for people with that kind of disease, we know that she was an outcast. She could not go to either a synagogue or the temple. She was excluded from her family. Her husband, if she had one, had every right to divorce her. She was considered untouchable. It was forbidden to touch her, her clothing, or anything she had contaminated by her contact.

We can imagine what happened to her inner conversation with herself about that through those long, excruciating years. Her self-esteem was the first to go, then her womanly dignity, and finally her self-respect. Think what you'd say to yourself if you were deemed untouchable, rejected by those you loved, and considered unclean by all society. That would debilitate your prayers, wouldn't it? I suspect the woman had reached the point of hopeless despair, where she no longer prayed. What's the use?

"If I Can Only See Jesus"

But at the lowest ebb of discouragement in her inner dialogue, a liberating thought arose. She had heard about Jesus and His mighty acts of healing. Could that happen to her if she could meet Him? But how could that happen? She was a lowly woman, an untouchable outcast at that. Then those doubting thoughts were challenged in her mind by the news that Jesus was coming across the Sea of Galilee and was about to land right there at Capernaum. An audacious, impelling compulsion formed in her talk with herself. *If I could only see Him! Is He what people have said? Full of love, care, concern, and compassion for people others have rejected?*

The news had spread. She knew of the man who had been cleansed of an unclean spirit in Capernaum, during Jesus' previous visit to the city. Simon Peter's mother had been healed of a high fever at the Master's word. A leper had been healed when He broke the rule against touching a person with the dreaded disease, threw aside all caution of contacting the disease, and actually took the man by the hand and healed him. Nothing seemed to hinder the healing power that flowed through Him. Even on the Sabbath. News of that was everywhere. A man with a withered hand had been healed in spite of the criticism and consternation of the Pharisees.

As the woman thought about all she had heard she felt a surge of hope within her. It was a thought, an emotion, and a desire, all at the same time. She had to see the Master. All that she had heard of Him had planted a seed of faith in her. She was amazed at herself, and as she talked with herself about Jesus' healing power and her need to be healed, reserve and reservation were cast aside. Somehow, some way, she had to get a look at Jesus of Nazareth. She pressed breathlessly, strangely hopeful, to the edge of the crowd.

When she saw Him step from the boat, the same surge of confidence and daring leaped within the woman. But now it was stronger. As she looked at Him from a distance, everything within her was drawn to Him. His whole countenance exuded love mingled with tender compassion. *Look at that face!* she said to herself. *Those eyes dancing with joy and vitality, that smile that winsomely communicates affirmation, that firm jaw of determined purpose!*

Suddenly she entertained a compelling thought. The healing power of God was in Jesus. She had heard about it. Now she knew it for herself. She could not dare interrupt Him. How could He give her time? And if He touched her, He could be deemed unclean. But if she could touch Him! *That's all it would take!* she thought.

When she looked at the Master again, He stood out against all the others. His commanding presence was dramatic; His white outer robe reflected the bright sun. Then she saw the four tassels connected by a blue thread to the hem of His robe, two on the front corners, and two on the back. They became the focus of the attention of her mind.

Did this troubled woman know the significance of the tassels? We wonder. They were a reminder of the law of God, clearly dictated by Numbers 15:37–41:

> Again the Lord spoke to Moses, saying, "Speak to the children of Israel: Tell them to make tassels on the corners of their garments throughout their generations, and to put a blue thread in the tassels of the corners. And you shall have the tassel, that you may look upon it and remember all the commandments of the Lord

and do them, and that you may not follow the harlotry
to which your own heart and your own eyes are in-
clined, and that you may remember and do all My
commandments, and be holy for your God. I am the
Lord your God, who brought you out of the land of
Egypt, to be your God: I am the Lord your God.

The same Lord God was present in Jesus Christ, and the
tassels He wore were not only an expression of His faithfulness
to the traditions of Israel, but also to the deliverance He was
enacting and would complete on the cross for the forgiveness
and liberation of His people from sickness.

As the woman stood at the edge of the crowd her growing
faith was mingled with the superstition that she could gain
healing by touching the Master's garment tassels. Then a moving thing happened that heightened her desire to make contact
with Him.

A ruler of the synagogue, named Jairus, pushed through the
crowd and fell down at Jesus' feet. The poignant words he
spoke cut through the air. His only daughter, twelve years old,
was dying. He begged the Master to come to his house. The
woman watched Jesus as He responded with tender compassion and then, with determination in His face, turned to follow
Jairus to his home. That's all it took. A passionate request, a
humble kneeling before the Master, and He responded. Surely
the power of Yahweh to heal was present. She had to follow
the crowd. Everything within her impelled her on. Then as she
followed, still at the edge of the crowd, her conversation with
herself quickened.

From Helplessness to Faith

Her thoughts had moved from her helplessness to reflection
on what Jesus had done to others, to His readiness to help

Jairus, and then to a firm conviction. Talking to herself, she repeated words that amazed her. *If I only may touch His garment, I will be made well.* Over and over she repeated the words, prompted by the mysterious gift of faith that compelled her forward.

When she could wait no longer, she began to push her way through the crowd, her eyes focused on the tassels of the Master's robe.

Now her outcast, untouchable status became a temporary blessing. As those in the crowd saw her they quickly stepped aside to avoid contact with her or the touch of her hand. A pathway was readily cleared by the fearful people.

Now the Master was in full view. She could see the back of His robe swaying as he walked. "If I can only touch Him!" she repeated as she stumbled along, trying to catch up with His striding pace. Nearer and nearer she came. Then she lunged forward. "A touch will do. All I need is a touch!" And then she grasped the tassel. In the very moment, a hot flash of spine-tingling, tissue-healing, hemorrhage-stopping power pulsed through her. The bleeding stopped. The woman knew she was healed.

Her conversation with herself suddenly took another turn. The Master had stopped in His tracks, standing motionless. *I must escape!* the woman thought. She tried to make her way back through the crowd. Then Jesus turned and said, "Who touched Me?"

The inner dialogue inside the disciples' minds reflected on this amazing, almost absurd question. Then Peter blurted out the wonderment they all had thought. "Master, the multitudes throng You and press You, and You say, 'Who touched Me?' " (Luke 8:45). Jesus did not acknowledge the amazement that expressed the lack of understanding of His sensitivity to individual need and of His awareness whenever the healing power of Yahweh was exercised through Him.

Jesus persisted with His concern. "Somebody touched Me, for I perceived power going out from Me" (Luke 8:46). He cast His eyes around the crowd, slowly searching out a face that would show the undeniable effects of receiving His power. Then His eyes met the woman's, and she knew that He knew it was she. She could not hide from the Master. Trembling, the woman made her way back through the crowd and fell at His feet.

Mark records that she told Him the "whole truth." What a magnificent phrase to describe what she must have said. She told Jesus all about herself, her sickness, the years of suffering, the ostracism, the loneliness, the helplessness. Then she raised her eyes, met His again, and she praised Him that her touch of His garment had healed her. Jesus' response acknowledged before the whole crowd, including Jairus, a ruler of the synagogue who had power to reinstate her as a healed woman, that she was indeed healed. The Lord's words carried the affirmation of healing and the brightness of her future as a restored person. "Daughter, be of good cheer; your faith has made you well. Go in peace" (Luke 8:48).

This is the only time Jesus called a woman "daughter." It was an expression of love and tenderness. But why *daughter* instead of *sister?* She was probably about His age or older. Could it be that it was with the authority of the Father He spoke? I think so. Remember the words we quoted that He spoke explaining the healing of the man by the pool. "Most assuredly, I say to you, the Son can do nothing of Himself, but what He sees the Father do; for whatever He does, the Son also does in like manner" (John 5:19). It was with the authority of Yahweh, Jehovah-Rapha, "the Lord is our Healer" that He spoke.

Faith: The Channel for Healing

Note carefully that Jesus identified the woman's faith as the channel through which the healing power of God had been released from Jesus into her body. Then don't miss the particularized caring of Jesus for one person in the thronging crowd. Finally, catch the full significance of the remedial words, "Go in peace," and what that would mean for the woman's future. These three emphases become the basis of what this account has to say to us in our quest to discover how to pray for ourselves when we need healing.

Consider first the way the woman's dialogue with herself about her needs was inspired by the infusion of the gift of faith. Faith does not begin or grow in a vacuum. It is not wishful thinking or self-induced positive expectation. Faith is a precious, diamondlike word that flashes in the total light of our understanding of the New Testament.

Faith is a gift. It is a seed that is planted and grows by exposure to the grace and truth of Jesus Christ. It is foolish to say to ourselves, or to anyone else, when we long for healing, "What is needed is more faith." Exposure to Christ comes first. When we encounter Him as triumphant Lord, faith is engendered in us. Never ask for more faith. Rather ask for more of Christ.

D. L. Moody once said that he prayed for years for more faith. In his own words:

> I prayed for faith as though someday faith would come down and strike me like lightning. But faith did not seem to come. One day I read the tenth chapter of Romans, "Faith cometh by hearing, and hearing by the Word of God." I had up to this time closed my Bible and prayed for faith. I now opened my Bible and began to study, and faith has been growing ever since.

The point for us is that when we long for healing in some area of our lives, it is absolutely absurd to try to have faith in faith. Faith is a by-product of beholding Christ, reading the gospels to witness His incarnate power, standing at the foot of the cross to receive His forgiveness through His atoning blood, claiming His resurrection and His present availability, and realizing that He is continuing to do in our time exactly what He did as Jesus of Nazareth.

Faith is released in us when our inner conversation with ourselves turns to prayer and we confess our abjèct need of His absolute authority over our lives. The Lord gives us that gift of faith to claim Him as Lord of our lives. The courage to press through the crowd and touch Him is enabled by Him as He waits to mediate His healing power to us.

How shall we understand Jesus' words to the woman, "Your faith has made you well"? It was faith prompted by Him, the knowledge of His mighty works, the discovery of His care for individuals, and by His magnificent presence. That changed the woman's inner rumination to resolve. As Alexander McLaren put it, "His mercy, like water, takes the shape of the containing vessel."

Jesus: A Loving, Compassionate Healer

But we don't have to wait for our faith to be perfected. The woman was convinced of one thing: Jesus was a loving, compassionate healer of people. She had so much less to go on than we have. We have the full biblical record of His power; we live on this side of Easter and Pentecost; and we have the evidence of two thousand years of His healing interventions in the lives of people. That sends us to prayer with the conviction and compulsion, "If I can only touch Him!"

And we can. He created the desire in us. He waits for us to

want Him more than healing. Then in blessed communion with Him, He releases His healing power. But the more we are with Him in prayer, the more we realize that He does not just *give* healing; He *is* healing. When we receive Him, we release our needs for His healing Spirit to infuse our minds, emotions, bodies, and attitudes. The extent to which we accept His gift of faith to trust Him completely—to that extent He will do for us what is ultimately best for us for now and eternity. In union with Him we are given what to ask and the quiet patience to receive according to His plan for us.

It is at this point that we must confront the negative attitude in ourselves and others, which is exemplified so vividly by the disciples in this account. How can the Lord know and care about all the people in need? I think the gospel writers included this story not only to stress the central role of the gift of faith in healing, but also to remind us that Jesus is eternally interruptible and available to anyone who persists with determination to make contact with Him.

If the eternal Logos who made us could feel the touch of faith by one person in a jostling crowd, during His incarnation, how much more is He aware of us now, on the edge of the crowd of prayers, seeking His help in any moment of time. As the glorified, reigning Christ, God with us still, to heal and make whole, He sees and knows when we press through the crowd and reach out for His help.

More than that, the Lord is the instigator of the desire. He is the inspiration of the idea that He is ready and able to help us. The stirring of desire to bring our needs to Him for healing originates with Him. His response when we finally reach out for Him is not, "Who touched Me?" but, "I've been waiting for you. I knew you'd finally turn to Me. Now trust Me with your need." Then in our hearts we fall on our knees and exclaim, "Lord, I believe, help my unbelief!"

And from then on our inner dialogue with ourselves is not, *If I could only touch Him* but a song of praise that He has touched us.

> Since I met this blessed Savior
> Since He cleansed and made me whole
> I will never cease to praise Him
> I'll shout it while eternity rolls.
> He touched me Oh, He touched me
> And oh, the joy that floods my soul
> Something happened and now I know,
> He touched me and made me whole.

But that's only the beginning. There's more—so much more. The touch is by a hand connected to everlasting arms that hold us and will not let us go.

Jesus Says to Us, "Go in Peace"

What the Lord said to the woman, He says to us, "Go in peace." The original really means, "Go into peace." The full promise of the deeper meaning of the Hebrew *shalom*, health of body and soul, is offered. It will be an ever-increasing experience.

The Lord does not touch one aspect of our lives and leave the rest unhealed. He enters the tissues of our brains to enable us to think His thoughts and look at life through His eyes. He heals debilitating memories and changes our self-images. He moves through our entire nervous systems, releasing our human energies coupled with His maximizing power. He fills our bodies with His strength. Jangled nerves become calm, tensed muscles relax, and our senses are utilized to appreciate the wonder of being fully alive. Most of all, our mental, emotional, and physical capabilities begin to function around the unifying command of His indwelling Spirit in us.

It doesn't happen all at once. Not usually, at least. We grow into peace. The Lord knits our fragmented natures into harmonious functioning. He's never finished with us. That's why He constantly motivates us to want to yield more of ourselves to Him. The peace He offers for today is nothing in comparison to what we will know tomorrow. Then we discover the secret of the healing of all our hurts and hopes. We don't need to strive to gain more of Him. He's offered all in His present, persistent, and penetrating Spirit. Our need is to allow Him to take hold of more of us!

That changes our inner conversation with ourselves with which we began this chapter. Now we ask, *What thoughts, habits, attitudes, goals, relationships, ambitions have I kept out of the reach of His healing touch?* The answer defines the next step of our growth into peace. And like all His blessings, the gift and the Giver can never be separated. They are one and the same. He is our healing and the peace that results.

What I've tried to communicate in this chapter is illustrated by a dear friend by the name of Jean. She responded to the invitation to come forward to pray with one of the elders of our church. She told him that she needed a fresh touch from the Lord. Jean had been enduring a long period of cancer treatment. She longed for the Lord's healing and courage. His answer to her appeal and the elder's prayer for her was not as immediate or as profound as she had expected. There was no quick remedying of the cancer, but weeks later a far greater healing took place.

For nearly eight years Jean had felt what she called a big boulder inside her stomach. It was a tremendous weight of guilt coupled with an inability to forgive. Her first husband had divorced her after years of marriage. She felt remorse, resentment, and hurt. After he left her, she became weighed down by this hard stone in her feelings. Her heartache rendered her incapable of acting and communicating with others on any deep level. The emotional pain made her want to scream most of the time.

When she subsequently remarried, the guilt over the failure of her first marriage made it difficult to express love and caring to her new husband.

Then she was diagnosed as having a serious form of cancer. The emotional distress had taken a form of physical malignancy. All this brought her to the chancel steps to ask for prayer.

One afternoon soon afterward, the Lord's answer to her prayer was given. The cold, heavy stone of emotional ache was lifted. No explanation, no startling insight. Suddenly it was gone. She realized the ache had dissipated and was totally removed. Jean knew she was forgiven and was able to forgive her first husband and the woman he had married, barely after the ink was dry on the divorce papers. The resentment she had carried dissolved.

The worry over her cancer had led her to ask for prayer. She wanted physical healing. The Lord intervened with a healing of the greater need in her. He healed her memory, emotions, and spirit. The amazing release she experienced greatly aided the healing of her cancer. Now she is healed of both the carcinoma and the dreadful emotional ache. She asked for one thing and received so much more. The Lord's grace became her sufficiency, and His perfect strength was given in response to her cry of weakness.

5 Putting People in Touch With the Master

One night as I lay awake praying I realized how many people in my life needed healing. As I mentally moved down my long list, I pictured the face of each person, focusing on the physical, emotional, or interpersonal need. I recognized how much I longed to bring these people to the Master, to have them receive what only He could give them.

You know how I felt. You, too, have felt the strange mixture of worry and concern about people that drives you to call out to the Lord for His healing touch in their lives. Most of the anxieties, troubles, and concerns in our lives have the same spelling: *p-e-o-p-l-e.*

People who face crippling malignancies, endure racking pain, or suffer with disabilities.

People who are troubled by what life has done to them or are filled with guilt over what they've done with life.

People whose lack of self-esteem has imprisoned them with self-limitations or people whose personalities have made them difficult to love.

People who are frustrated by the reverses of their plans and hopes and are about to give up.

People who have lost loved ones, and their hearts sob with grief too painful to contain and too personal to express.

When our hearts become burdened with the needs of others, we ask one of life's most urgent questions. Not just, "Why do bad things happen to good people?" but, "How can we get the people about whom we are concerned in touch with the Master?"

That night as I prayed I became aware that not only was I concerned about people in trouble, but most of all about those who were troubled with their concerns for people. Their questions about how to pray for people in need tumbled around in my mind. After what seemed to be hours of intercessory prayer, I fell asleep.

The Dream

I had a dream that was as vivid when I awoke as when I dreamed it. I dreamed that as I finished a sermon one Sunday morning, a voice thundered in the sanctuary. It was the voice of the Lord! What He said startled and amazed the people. "I will appear here next Sunday. I will be available for all the people to bring to Me the person in their lives about whom they are most concerned, and I will heal them."

My dream spanned the next week of excited preparation. News of the Lord's promise spread throughout the congregation and, because our services are televised, across the nation. On the Saturday before the promised appearance, the Los Angeles airport was jammed with people coming from all over the nation for the wondrous event. Early on Sunday morning, before dawn, the sanctuary was filled to capacity, and people lined up outside, waiting to get in. Traffic congested the freeways and streets for miles around.

At the appointed time of the first service, we all waited expectantly. The usual order of worship seemed cumbersome and the customary procedures irrelevant for an appearance of the Lord. People waited with anticipation, each grasping the hand of the person he or she had brought to put in touch with the Master. The sick, lame, and troubled were evident everywhere.

Then it happened. No physical appearance. Just the same voice, filled with love and compassion. "Lo, I am with you always!" the Master said. Nothing more. An awesome, breathless silence fell over the congregation. Then a man in the balcony began to sing with reverent intensity, "He is Lord, He is Lord. He is risen from the dead, and He is Lord. Every knee shall bow, and every tongue confess, that Jesus Christ is Lord!" The people in the sanctuary and all those crowded around outside in the streets began to join the song of praise. People streamed down the aisles, hand in hand with those who needed healing, and knelt on the chancel steps. The procession of human need flowed forth throughout the morning, on into the afternoon, and until late at night. When I awoke, a profound peace pervaded me. It was a dramatic contrast to the fitful distress I'd felt when I went to sleep.

The Lord: Always Available, Always Interruptible

The dream needs little interpretation. The Lord had used it to impress me again with His availability, so much greater than any physical manifestation. The Lord is continuing His healing ministry. We can know more of Him and realize more of His power than those who stood beside Him in the flesh watching Him heal the sick of body and soul.

Several things gripped my mind. The Lord is always interruptible. He cares more about the people for whom we are concerned than we do. He takes the intercessory prayers we pray and answers by healing the deepest needs in people. My dream had relieved me of the necessity of trying to get the Master's attention for the people I knew needed His healing. I didn't need to convince Him about what was the human diagnosis or prognosis. He is both omniscient and omnipresent. He knows every need before we pray. But He has so ordered the release of His healing power to be given in response to prayers of love prayed with faith and boldness. Our only task is to bring people to Him and place them before His gracious, tender, all-powerful healing presence.

That was the urgent desire of four men in Capernaum during one of Jesus' visits there (Luke 5:18–25; Mark 2:1–12). They had heard about the Master's healing of a man with an unclean spirit during a previous visit. The news of the Nazarene's healing miracles elsewhere had reached them. The blind were given sight, the lame walked, and the troubled were given comfort and courage. Now Jesus was there with them in their city again. A friend of theirs desperately needed His healing touch. He was paralyzed, unable to walk. They had to get him to Jesus! How they did it and how the Master responded are filled with powerful insight for us. The story gives us guidelines for our ministry of intercessory prayers for healing.

Picture the scene. Jesus was preaching and teaching inside one of the small houses that lined the streets of Capernaum. It was a one-room, boxlike structure. On the top of stone walls was a roof made of saplings, bound together with sand, pitch, and mud. Over that tiles were laid.

Inside the house, Jesus was surrounded by scribes and Pharisees who were listening closely to His message—not so much to be inspired by the truth He proclaimed as to entrap Him with any regulation He might deny. Around these officials, who had judgment and consternation written on their faces, was a crowd of people with expectation and hope in their eyes. The crowd packed the room and flowed out into the court outside. Many people jostled for a place by the door, to get a look at the Master.

A Daring Plan

When the four men arrived at the edge of the crowd, carrying their friend on a cot, they were overcome with the seeming impossibility of getting him before the Master. They had to find a way; they would not be put off by the crowd or dissuaded by the difficulties. A plan was devised. They would carry their friend up the side steps of the house and onto the roof. Then they would break through the roof and lower down their friend before Jesus.

Imagine what happened from the perspective of those inside the house gathered around the Master. Get inside the skin of one of the religious leaders or one of the teeming crowd. See what took place first through their ears and then through their eyes.

A persistent pounding on the roof and then the sound of tiles being ripped apart interrupted Jesus' teaching. Everyone looked up, impatient with the distraction. Jesus paused and then continued His message. Suddenly the ceiling of the room cracked, and sand and splinters of wood, mingled with pieces of tile, showered down on Jesus, the religious leaders, and the crowd.

Then a man's clenched fist punched its way through the ceiling. The people were astounded. The hole made by the fist was widened progressively as eight hands tore away the roof. Surprise left the people motionless, unable to grasp what was happening. The opening grew wider, until it was about three feet wide and over six feet long. What were these men doing?

Picture the expressions on the faces of the men who had broken through the roof when they peered down through the opening. They quickly surveyed the crowd and then fastened their eyes on Jesus. Did He smile approvingly? They nodded to one another and then lifted the cot with their immobilized friend stretched out on it. With ropes attached to the four corners, they centered the cot over the gaping hole and proceeded to lower their friend down in front of the Master.

Don't miss the look on Jesus' face as He watched the stretcher slowly descend. His eyes twinkled with delight over the concern expressed by the four men, and then His look softened with the moist warmth of compassion for the man on the cot as the sick man's face descended into view and his frail body was placed at the Master's feet. The man looked up at Jesus imploringly. And in response, all the love and power incarnate in the Master surged in reaction to the man's physical immobility and his friends' persistence.

There was a long pause before Jesus spoke. With divine discernment He not only looked at the man's prolonged physical plight but also into the depths of his soul. Jesus saw a deeper need than just the healing of his rigid body. The man needed God, forgiveness, and a healing of his spirit. What the Master said after His prayerful silence surprised the man's four friends, alarmed the religious leaders, and astounded the people in the crowd. *In direct response to the faith expressed by the man's friends,* Jesus said, "Man, your sins are forgiven you" (Luke 5:20).

A stir rippled through the crowd. The four men on the roof, leaning through the hole, looked at one another with wonderment. They had wanted their friend to be healed, not forgiven. The scribes and the Pharisees turned to one another with agitation and disdain. "Who is this who speaks blasphemies? Who can forgive sins but God alone?"

Jesus knew what they were saying. His response to them rang with messianic authority. "Why are you reasoning in your hearts? Which is easier, to say, 'Your sins are forgiven you,' or to say, 'Rise up and walk'?" (Luke 5:22, 23).

The point was, neither was easy. Only God could do either. And in the Son of Man the forgiving authority and healing power of God were incarnate—God in human form. Boldly asserting who He was, Jesus gave the paralyzed soul and body of the man both forgiveness and healing, saying, "But that you may know that the Son of Man has power on earth to forgive sins, . . . I say to you, arise, take up your bed, and go to your house" (Luke 5:24). The man leaped up, liberated from his paralysis, and began glorifying God for the miracle of forgiving love and physical healing. No wonder Luke tells us, "And they were all amazed, and they glorified God and were filled with fear, saying, 'We have seen strange things today!' " (Luke 5:26). Indeed they had. Wondrous things!

What had happened was a wonderful foreshadowing and promise of why the Lord had come and what was ahead of Him in the fulfillment of His purpose. He would go to the cross to suffer for the sins of the whole world. After the resurrection, ascension, and return in the Spirit, He would continue His ministry. A cross, an open tomb, and an upper room crowded with Christ-filled disciples and followers would be the undeniable evidence of His all-encompassing healing ministry. And down through the ages He has continued to do what He did that day in Capernaum. Whenever we lower before Him the people about whom we are concerned, He will forgive and heal with the authority of the risen, all-powerful, reigning Lord. He is the same today and forever.

Insights About Praying for Others

This account of the healing of the paralyzed man is filled with helpful insights about how to pray for people who need healing.

FAITH. Consider that it was the *faith* of the four men who brought their friend to Jesus that motivated His response. Today He honors our faith in placing people before Him. But that faith does not grow in a vacuum. It is engendered through our own relationship with the Savior. Faithful intercessory prayers are offered by those who have experienced spiritual and physical healing in their own lives.

Faith, as we discussed in the previous chapter, is a gift from the Lord Himself and grows through consistent fellowship with Him. As we surrender our own needs and experience the timely interventions of the Lord, we long to share His power with others. If you've slacked off in prayers for others, it's probably a sign that your relationship with the Lord has become perfunctory and aloof.

The Lord wants to bind us together in mutual concerns. The longer I live and seek to understand the spiritual laws undergirding intercessory prayer, the more I am convinced that the Lord often patiently waits to bless us or intervene in our needs until we pray for each other. He is consistently drawing us to Himself and to each other. Prayer for each other binds us to one another.

Recently a pastor called me asking how to begin an intercessory prayer program in his church. My response startled the man. "Is there an authentic renewal of faith taking place in your church?" I asked. "That's the place to begin. Help your officers and members to surrender their own needs to the Lord. Exciting things will begin to happen. Faith will be quickened, and then people will want to pray for others. You can't motivate an intercessory prayer movement until people are excited about what the Lord is doing in their own lives. Prayer for others follows naturally."

The man had planned to try to convince his people that they "ought" to be more concerned and pray for people's healing. He was starting at the wrong end. What he needed was a fresh Pentecost in his church, in which his people received power. Renewed people become prayer warriors. They can't help it. Their revitalized faith makes prayer for the healing of others the passion of their lives.

Careful study of the New Testament reveals that there are really two levels of faith.

The first is a Spirit-induced gift to believe in Christ as our Lord and Savior. This is essential faith.

The second quality of faith is wonder-working faith that is given us for specific needs and challenges. Paul speaks of this faith as a gift of the Holy Spirit in 1 Corinthians 12. The same Spirit who gives us faith to say that Jesus is Lord (v. 3) also gives a special endowment of daring faith to envision and claim what the Lord desires in a particular situation or person's life.

This understanding of two levels of faith heightens our understanding of the great need among so many Christians today. They have faith in Christ for salvation, but have not received the spiritual gift of bold faith. Note that Paul lists the gift of faith immediately following the gifts of wisdom and knowledge (1 Corinthians 12:7–9). That shows us the progression of how the Lord prepares us for intercessory prayer. He gives us wisdom to know His plan and purpose. Then He gives us knowledge, the practical application of what He has revealed He desires in a person's life. After that He gives us the courage to ask in faith, believing that which He has helped us picture in our imaginations.

All these gifts are offered you and me right now. Without them we will seldom be motivated to pray for the manifold dimensions of healing the Lord desires to give, and what we pray until we are thus gifted will often miss the mark of the miracle the Lord intends.

THE LORD'S ANSWER. A powerful truth about intercessory prayer revealed in this account of the healing of the paralytic is that *the Lord answers our prayers for others at the point of their deepest need,* not at the level of our desires. He knows and understands the people for whom we pray so much better than we do. So often our prayers for people are circumstantial or situational. We ask for the resolution of problems, for guidance in decisions, or for healing in physical or emotional illness. These may not be the most profound needs.

The Lord penetrates to the core of the inner condition of our souls. He is magnificently original in the ways He deals with the people for whom we pray. In some cases, He uses the very problem we asked to be resolved to bring the person into deeper trust in Him. Or He may time the blessing so that the person can praise Him for it and move on to greater growth. All we need to know is that the Lord is the Healer, and He will answer our prayers according to His timing and plan, if we will simply place people before Him in complete surrender of their needs to Him. The Lord's timetable and agenda are so much better than ours. Evelyn Greenway expresses this in a beautiful way:

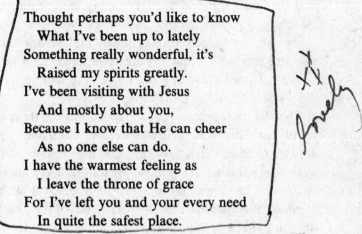

Thought perhaps you'd like to know
  What I've been up to lately
Something really wonderful, it's
  Raised my spirits greatly.
I've been visiting with Jesus
  And mostly about you,
Because I know that He can cheer
  As no one else can do.
I have the warmest feeling as
  I leave the throne of grace
For I've left you and your every need
  In quite the safest place.

When Jesus forgave the paralytic's sins before He healed him, He simply affirmed the close relationship of the spiritual and physical. Note that He did not say that this man's paralysis was caused by sin. Rather the Master dealt with *both* his spiritual and physical disability. He does both for us and the people for whom we pray.

We all have sins that need to be forgiven. As we have said, sin is to miss the mark, to be separated in any area of our lives from the Lord, or to willfully do what is contrary to the Ten Commandments or the greater commandment to love the Lord and our neighbor as ourselves. The independence of running our own lives is the basic sin that gets us into all the lesser sins. And there'll always be some sin we need to confess. When we do, we are freed of any encumbrance blocking our physical healing. The same is true for the people for whom we pray.

GLORIFYING GOD. Another aspect of this healing miracle of
the paralytic is that he and the people *glorified God.* I suspect
that the greatest praise from the people came from those four
stretcher bearers on the roof. No one praised them for their he-
roic persistence. Good thing. They might have taken credit for
enabling the miracle and lost their effectiveness for future feats
of faith. There's no limit to what the Lord will do for the people we love if we give Him the glory.

The other day I remarked to a man about the transformation
in his son. The young man had been through a long period of
rebellion and eccentric behavior. The man responded to my affirmation of his son by saying, "He'd never have made it without his mother's and my prayers!" No word of praise to the
Lord, only self-acclaim for the persistence of their prayers. We
are not to have faith in prayer, but in the Lord who hears and
answers prayer.

Praise for past answers strengthens our intercessory prayer
muscles for future trust of new needs as they emerge. The Lord
delights to bless the intercessor who has shown his willingness
to pass on the credit to Him. So often we are engulfed in new
problems and forget to thank the Lord for what He's done in
previous ones.

In our congregation, we encourage our people to spend at
least the first five minutes of their morning devotions in glorifying the Lord for the blessings of the previous day. That keeps
us up-to-date in our praise and gratitude. Often I begin my
morning quiet time singing the old gospel song, "Count your
blessings—name them one by one; Count your many blessings—see what God has done." I change the last few words;
"And it will delight you what the Lord will do!" It doesn't
rhyme, but it does keep my focus on the crucial relationship of
praise for the past and being a joyous receiver in the future.

Also, glorifying the Lord prior to the resolution of needs in people for whom we pray is an ultimate, liberating level of trust in intercessory prayer. I know it works. When I thank the Lord for hearing my prayer and answering according to His will, I am able to really let go of worry and concern. That praise also frees us to receive what the Lord ordains, even when it's not what *we* thought best.

All this becomes very personal when we actually enact in our minds what happened there that day in Capernaum. Put the person about whom you are most concerned on that stretcher. Picture him or her placed before the Master. Surrender the person to Him completely. Let go of your management of that person. The Lord knows your faith and will release His healing for him or her at the deepest level of need. Now glorify the Lord that His healing miracle has already begun.

6 Overcoming Negative Attitudes

One of the most positive people I've ever met was the late E. Stanley Jones, the dynamic missionary and author. Some years ago, this winsome man in Christ was a guest in our home and a speaker in our church, when I was a pastor in Bethlehem, Pennsylvania. It was exciting to spend a few, brief days with him. His positive attitude was communicated in every conversation and sparkled in every message he gave. I asked him for the reason behind this positive attitude toward life. His response was, "I believe in Jesus Christ as Lord of my life and have surrendered all that I am and have to His authority!"

When it was time for him to press on to his next speaking engagement, I took him to the airport. Though in his eighties, he climbed the steps to the airplane with the vigor of a twenty-year-old. Just before he entered the door of the plane, he turned back and waved to me. He made a customary gesture for which he had become known. He raised three fingers of his hand, one for each of the three words that empowered and guided his energetic life: "Jesus is Lord!"

A brief time afterward, this dynamic disciple of the Lord was stricken with a crippling stroke. At eighty-nine, Dr. Jones faced one of the most difficult battles of his life. Yet he was determined to regain his speech and walk again. Even though the paralysis persisted, he maintained a positive attitude rooted in his unassailable trust in Jesus as Lord. He prayed and asked people all over the world to pray that he would walk again. An around-the-clock prayer vigil was marshaled. And Jones insisted that anytime he was awakened from sleep that the nurse or friend attending him speak the energizing admonition, "In the name of Jesus of Nazareth, rise and walk."

During his five months in a Boston hospital, Dr. Jones used a tape recorder to chart his progress back to normalcy of speech. Then he began to dictate a book to add to the many he had already published. The title of the book he began to compose expressed the attitude that distinguished his life: *The Divine Yes.*

The indefatigable prayer warrior and communicator of hope wherever he went revealed his secret of power in that title. All through his life, as a missionary in India and later as a peripatetic evangelist all over the world, E. Stanley Jones sought the Lord's Spirit in the conditioning of his thought. The Lord's "yes!" was persistently what he longed for most of all in daily guidance and the strategy of his ministry. His confidence in the Lord's power and his surrender to His authority produced an attitude of "yes!" to the unlimited possibilities of what He could and would do in problems and perplexities. All through the process of recuperation from his stroke, he remained positive. During this period he wrote, "I haven't had a blue moment yet!"

When Dr. Jones was taken to the Himalayas in his beloved India to further recuperate, he persisted in his positive response to the "divine yes." Finally he was able to walk again and resume his impelling preaching of Christ as Lord. He remained strong in his faith and preached victorious living in Christ until the day when this portion of his eternal life was completed and he went to join his positive voice with the adoration of the company of heaven.

E. Stanley Jones's inner conviction that Jesus is Lord was the source of his outward expression—his positive attitude of "yes!" to the Lord. In active ministry or in recovering from illness, that attitude opened the floodgates of his mind, will, emotions, and body to the inflow of the Spirit of Christ.

Attitudes: Their Awesome Effect

I want to investigate with you the awesome effect our attitudes have on aiding or debilitating the healing power of Christ in us or the people around us.

Attitudes are congealed convictions. They are outer expressions of our inner thoughts. Our perception of what's happening to or around us is expressed in our actions, words, facial expressions, and body language. Positive attitudes encourage and speed up healing and recovery from illness. Negative attitudes, rooted in doubt or unbelief, actually cripple our healing. The will to get well and to trust in Christ's healing power in our bodies is absolutely necessary. Without it our brain sends the wrong signals to our nervous system and frustrates the healing process.

In the same way, our negative attitudes about the illnesses of loved ones and friends make their battle to recover twice as difficult. Our lack of conviction about Christ's healing power creates an attitude that becomes a burden to a person struggling to get well. Try as we will to camouflage them, our eyes express the thoughts our mouths would not dare to speak. An attitude of fear or doubting resignation will flash the message that's compressed in the confusion of our thinking brain.

That alarms us. What can we do with negative attitudes in the face of sickness in ourselves and others? Thought conditioning games seldom help. Nor do efforts to deny the existence of our own or others' problems. Negativism is the result of seeing things as they are and realizing we are impotent to change them.

On the other hand, authentic, positive attitudes in the midst of illness are the result of knowing Christ as the healing power of the world. But more than that, they are the result of putting ourselves under His authority in all of life. Many who believe in Christ have never surrendered to His authority. It is difficult to receive His authority over our sickness if our lives are still under our own authority. When sickness strikes, we cry out for help and healing without wanting His authority over our total selves.

This is not to imply that all people who get sick are resisting Christ's authority. Nor does it mean that everyone who must wait for healing is secretly refusing His authority over them. What it does mean is that total surrender of our lives produces a positive attitude in which Christ can do His miracles of healing (immediate or prolonged) in our bodies. Complete commitment results in the firm conviction that the Lord is in charge. We can relax and receive His healing in the way and in the time He wills. Lack of trust in Him as our healer slows up or blocks His Spirit's work in us.

Once again we return to actual examples from Jesus' ministry as the biblical basis of our thinking. There are two accounts that reveal the awesome power of attitudes in people affecting the healing ministry of the Lord. The centurion who asked for the healing of his servant displays the power of positive attitudes; the people of Jesus' hometown of Nazareth expose the limiting result of negative attitudes. Jesus was the same in both instances, and His authority to heal was equally available. The attitudes of people in each case mysteriously determined what Christ was willing to do. Let's look at both situations carefully, drawing some implications for our lives today.

A Positive Attitude Based on Faith

In Matthew 8:5–13 and Luke 7:1–10 we have two accounts of a centurion's appeal for Jesus to heal his servant. The Matthew passage has him come to Jesus himself, and the Luke passage says that the elders of the synagogue came on his behalf. The difference of the method of the appeal is not significant. What is significant is the appeal. It expresses a positive attitude based on faith in Jesus and His power to heal.

Blending both accounts about the centurion, we are able to paint a word portrait of him. He was a Roman officer over a hundred legionnaires. During his assignment in Palestine, he had been introduced to the Hebrew religion and became what was called a God-fearer, one who espoused belief in the God of the Hebrews, but had not been fully initiated into full Hebraism by circumcision and complete observance to the law and rituals of Moses. He loved the nation of Israel and had built a synagogue.

Accepting Christ's Authority

The centurion obviously had observed Jesus and known of His miracles and His mighty works. When his servant became ill, he immediately turned to Jesus for help. As a Roman officer he understood and respected authority. He had been trained to live under authority and to exercise authority over those under his command. That was a great advantage. He observed Jesus to be one in authority. He had witnessed the authority the Lord exercised in His power over sickness. He honored that display of delegated authority from God and was willing to place his life and the healing of his servant under that authority.

Note the vibrant confidence the centurion expresses in Christ's authority. When Jesus responded to his appeal for help for his paralyzed, tormented servant by saying, "I will come and heal him," the centurion exposed the convictions that were congealed in his positive attitude:

> Lord, I am not worthy that You should come under my roof. But only speak a word, and my servant will be healed. For I also am a man under authority, having soldiers under me. And I say to this one, "Go," and he goes; and to another, "Come," and he comes; and to my servant, "Do this," and he does it.
>
> Matthew 8:8, 9

Jesus marveled at this acceptance of His authority and gave the centurion an amazing statement of affirmation: "Assuredly, I say to you, I have not found such great faith, not even in Israel!" (Matthew 8:10). And then, in response to the request for the healing of the servant, Jesus said, "Go your way; and as you have believed, so let it be done for you" (Matthew 8:13).

The centurion's servant was healed at a distance at the very moment Jesus exercised His authority over the sickness that had disabled him. Note the healing was transmitted without physical contact. That assures us that distance from the people for whom we pray makes little difference. The power of Christ to heal is available through His authoritative command. And how much more now, when His Spirit motivates us to pray and at the same time activates the answer. That is, if we have the crucial element of a dynamic faith that produces a truly positive attitude toward what He is able and ready to do.

What was it in the centurion's faith that exceeded any evidence of faith Jesus had found in all of Israel? Remember that would have included the disciples, others who had received healing, and the great host of Jesus' many followers at that time. The centurion's words expose the dynamic quality, "For I am also a man under authority, having soldiers under me." Being under authority and having authority, he could understand and accept Jesus' authority under God and over the forces of evil and the power of sickness. He could place himself and his servant's sickness under Christ's authority. That's it! The element of the centurion's faith in Christ, surpassing the faith of anyone else Jesus had found in all of Israel, was submission to His authority. That submission created the context in which Jesus was willing to heal the man's servant.

Surrender to Christ's authority is the essential ingredient of faith that produces the kind of "Why not?" expectant trust that is the theme of this book. Consistent, daily commitment to Christ's authority over our minds produces the quality of confident thinking about what He is able to do that results in a positive attitude toward all of life.

A Negative Attitude: Unbelief and Distrust

Let us consider what happened to Jesus when He went to His hometown of Nazareth. He taught in the synagogue, and according to both Matthew and Mark (Matthew 13:53–58; Mark 6:1–6) He healed a few of His townspeople. The responses of His neighbors who had known Him for the thirty years prior to beginning His ministry were astonishment and unbelief. ". . . Where did this Man get this wisdom and these mighty works?" And then in faithless familiarity with the One who had been their community carpenter, they exclaimed, "Is this not the carpenter's son? Is not His mother called Mary? And His brothers James, Joses, Simon, and Judas? And His sisters, are they not all with us? Where did this Man get all these things?" (Matthew 13:54–56).

To this doubt and lack of faith Jesus spoke the oft-quoted words of analysis about human resistance to authority rooted in their own self-distrust. "A prophet is not without honor except in his own country and in his own house" (v. 57). The people could not imagine that one of their own people could do what Jesus did.

Nathaniel's question about Jesus before he met the Master face-to-face could have been spoken by the people of Jesus' hometown expressing their own lack of self-esteem: "Can any good come out of Nazareth?"

Matthew and Mark state flatly the result of the people's unwillingness to recognize Jesus' authority. Matthew puts it, "And He did not do many mighty works there because of their unbelief" (v. 58). And Mark spells out the same sad conclusion, "Now He could do no mighty work there, except that He laid His hands on a few sick people and healed them" (v. 5). Note that both accounts say that the Master could do no mighty works, and Mark says that He healed a few people.

I've often wondered about the difference indicated between the lack of mighty works and a few healings. Would not even one healing have been a mighty work? Surely, but Mark is talking about either the quantity of healings or something even more profound than that. <u>Perhaps what was lacking was the mighty work of the transformation of doubt into faith.</u> The people could not believe that one of their own townspeople could be God's Son, endowed with such wisdom and power. And behind that doubt was the unwillingness to submit to Jesus' authority as the Messiah.

Unlike the centurion, the people of Nazareth were neither under authority nor in authority. They had resisted God's authority in their lives and were misusing the responsibility He had entrusted to them to live for His glory. They suffered a common delusion with all Israel: They rejected God's authority in their lives through the most subtle but arrogant of defenses—religion, rules, and regulations. A prior time when Jesus had visited Nazareth (Luke 4:16–30), He read the pointed messianic passage from Isaiah 61:1, 2 and declared that the prophecy was fulfilled in Him. That time, they drove Him out of the city with disdain. Rejecting God's authority, their minds were closed to One who clearly claimed to be sent from Him.

Therefore, in contrast to the faith rooted in submission to Christ's authority exemplified by the centurion, the people of Nazareth were so negative about what Jesus could do that the mighty works He did elsewhere were not done among them.

Faith was engendered in people wherever Jesus went, except in His hometown. The Spirit of the Lord was as present there during Jesus' visit as He had been in other places. Elsewhere the Master's life and message stirred people deeply, and the Spirit of the Lord endowed them with faith to believe in Him. Those who did were healed and released from the bondage of sin or sickness. Not so in Nazareth. They could not submit to Jesus' authority. As a result, they expressed negative attitudes about what He could do for their own physical and spiritual needs.

Drawing on the insight of these two accounts—the centurion and the people of Nazareth—we discover the deeper causes of our negative attitudes, not only about life, ourselves, and the people around us, but also about the possibility of the Lord's healing power.

Rejecting Christ's Authority

My thesis is that negative people are those who refuse to submit to authority and resist taking authority. Allow me to explain what I mean. Many of us live under our own authority. We run the show. We determine our own goals, set our own priorities, and depend essentially on our own strength. We resist authority over us on a human level and tenaciously reject the Lord's authority in our lives.

When we face life's challenges and difficulties and do not have what it takes, we become aware of the unreliability of ourselves as our authority and source of strength or wisdom. We become distrustful of our own ability to measure up to life's demands. That's covered by defensiveness. We take on a general negativism about life and people. They are no more to be trusted than we are.

When there's no greater authority than our control and no power beyond what we can muster, we have little confidence in positive possibilities in life's opportunities or problems. We become like the people of Nazareth: We have no viable faith to expect or receive what the Lord is ready and able to do. We will not submit to His authority in our own lives and therefore cannot experience the authority He can exercise over the forces of evil, sickness, or despair around or in us. Unlike E. Stanley Jones, we say, "No!" to the divine "Yes!"

But the purpose of this chapter is not to be negative about people with negative attitudes. Rather it is to emphasize by contrast the positive attitudes of those who have placed themselves under Christ's authority and therefore experience His authority over sickness.

Surrendering Sickness to Christ's Authority

A dear friend of mine is presently undergoing cancer treatment. Years ago, she surrendered to Christ's authority and invited Him to live in her. This did not make her exempt from a physical illness, but it did give her the kind of positive attitude that has greatly expedited the healing process. With confidence in the Lord, she asked for the prayers of her friends. We have claimed her healing and thanked the Lord in advance for it, in His timing and way. "I am being healed!" is her consistent confidence. The doctors are astounded by her progress, way ahead of their schedule.

Years of living under the Lord's authority has enabled this woman to commit her sickness to Christ's authority to heal. She believes in the powerful authority of the name of Jesus Christ. The mysterious linkage between the mind and the body is affirmed. Her clear thinking about Christ's authority is sending the kind of signals that are releasing in her body the healing agents to combat her sickness. This coupled with the actual healing Spirit of Christ is bringing her back to complete health.

So often in caring for people who are ill, I have found that the turning point in their healing takes place when they surrender their plight to the Lord, relinquish their tenacious grip on their future, and relax in complete trust. The remarkable change that takes place is first manifested in their attitudes.

They become positive about the Lord's power in their lives. That releases all the potential healing resources of the body to be utilized by the Lord in getting well.

One of the reasons many of us miss that release of healing power is that we want to be sure of the results. So often we neglect bold prayers in Jesus' name, expecting His healing, because we are not sure He will act in the way we want, when we want it. The spirit of unbelief pervades our culture and infects our minds. The fear and panic about sickness make us helpless victims. We expect the worst and steel ourselves for its eventual occurrence.

Then in times of illness we realize how much we need the Lord's comfort and assurance. So we pray for His strength to endure. We are afraid to pray for healing because we fear we will be disappointed. Then where will we be? The last, frail thread of trust will be frayed and broken. That, too, is an effort to remain in charge, under our own control.

Putting our total life under the control of the Master is allowing Him to work out the results according to His plan. After all, we belong to Him whether we live or die. And as we will discuss later, death is only a transition in the midst of eternal life. But in the meantime, the physical problems we face are to be committed to the Lord, placed under His authority, and released for His disposition as He deems best.

In our prayers for others, being under Christ's authority is a mysterious prerequisite to being a healing agent. The centurion proved that. When we know how to accept authority, we can exercise it in our prayers.

A Healing Church

A church that is consistently faithful to commit its life, program, and direction to the Lord can be a healing church. When pastors, officers, and members surrender their lives together to Christ, He releases His power for healing. Miracles begin to happen. People are converted, lives are changed, and healing abounds.

A healing ambience results. A positive attitude pervades the worship, classes, and small groups. Condemnation and judgment are replaced by a joyous affirmation of the Lord's presence and power. That frees people to relinquish their tight control on their lives and experience the release of trusting their problems to the Lord.

Support groups for mutual care and encouragement for the sustaining of positive attitudes are rooted in convictions of Christ's control. We all need people who are positive about what the Lord can do with our difficulties. When we meet consistently for Bible study, sharing of needs, and mutual prayer, in the ambience of confident faith, we feel we are not alone, and the positive, expectant trust of the others in the group sets us free from crippling worry and fear.

A man in our congregation experienced the impact of a positive men's fellowship and prayer group. He was combating a chronic illness when he joined the group. Many of the men in the group had gone through the transformation of their attitudes, and they saw immediately that the man was his own worst enemy. Though he had been in the church and a Christian for years, he was a person driven by his own needs and was not under Christ's control.

The members of the group shared what had happened to them when they surrendered their lives and problems to the Lord. Their joyous, confident attitudes impressed the man. He wanted what they had. Layer by layer, they helped him unpeel the defensive protection he had built up around his soul. When his illness peaked in a physical crisis, the group visited him around the clock, invading his gloomy attitude with the radiance of their confidence in the Lord. His negative thinking was inhibiting the effectiveness of his immune system.

One day the group gathered around him and laid hands on him, praying for healing in the name of Jesus Christ. He felt a power surge through him as a tangible sign of the Lord's Spirit releasing him from pain. After that he started to get well. The doctor's treatment and the medication were maximized. The more positive he became, the stronger was his conviction to trust Christ's control of the future. His new attitude of hope and faith released responses in his adrenal cortex and boosted the effectiveness of his immune system. Christ, through the ministry of the positive attitudes of his fellow adventurers, had liberated the man's negative commitment to be sick the rest of his life and liberated him through a new commitment to Christ's control of the future, whatever happened.

Sadly, just the opposite is happening to a woman with whom I talked the other day. She, too, is battling sickness, but is surrounded by a family possessed with negativism rooted in fear and self-centered concern. Up until the time she became ill, this lady was the rock of the entire family. When she became ill, her husband and grown children fell apart emotionally. Their fear of losing her manifested itself in inordinate grimness. "I'm waging two battles," she said, "one against the sickness and the other against the negative attitudes of my family. How can I get well when they are so afraid I won't?"

That challenges us to reflect on our own attitudes toward sickness and loved ones and friends who are ill. Are we an added burden or an uplifting boost? Our commitment to Christ's authority will determine whether our attitudes are positive or negative.

Christ is alive, present with us, and has the same authority He exercised over sickness when He was Jesus of Nazareth. That healing can be received to the fullest when we trust Him completely, believe all things are possible through Him, and allow Him to transform our thinking and our whole attitude toward life.

I'm not sure about you, but this investigation of the powerful impact of our attitudes for our own and others' healing and health has made me wonder: Am I more like the people of Nazareth or the centurion? And that leads me to want to pray:

> Lord, You have all authority in heaven and on earth. I submit my life to Your authority. Possess my mind with clear convictions that You are in charge of my life and the lives of those about whom I am concerned. I surrender myself and them to You. Now, Lord, may that commitment result in a new, positive attitude that exudes joy and hope about the present and the future. In Your impossibility-defying name, Amen.

7 The Healing of Memories

The world stood at attention. Admiration mingled with wonderment. As television cameras brought the historic event into our homes, a deep longing in all of us was stirred, mysteriously touched.

Our hearts, steeled and cold because of unforgiven memories of what people have said and done to us, were strangely softened and warmed. A longing within us, pressed down and ignored by our own indignant sense of self-righteous judgment, was let loose and once again walked the corridors of hope and possibility in our minds.

Admiration for what a great man had done suddenly shifted to become a challenge to deal with our unfinished agenda of hurts stored in our hearts.

Pope John Paul II had gone to the top-security Rebebbia

prison in Rome and spent twenty-one minutes in an isolation cell with a prisoner he called his brother. The man was Ali Agca, the Turkish terrorist who had made an assassination attempt on the pope's life two and a half years before. The assassin's shots had lodged three bullets in the pontiff's abdomen, finger, and elbow, sending the spiritual leader to the hospital for many weeks, to recover from his scrape with death.

Now fully recovered, the pope had to deal with a far more serious wound. Another human being, filled with hatred, had wanted to kill him. The assassin was now locked in a well-guarded prison. The pope had to deal with a prison of a very different kind—the prison of memory. Though he had publicly declared to the world, from his hospital bed, that he had forgiven the terrorist, something further was required by the Lord whom John Paul serves as bishop of Rome, spiritual leader of millions of Roman Catholics, and admired example to all Christians. In his own prayers the pontiff had forgiven the man who had tried to kill him; then he told the world he had forgiven him; now he had to tell the man himself.

The zoom lenses of the cameras captured the intensity of the encounter—John Paul and Ali Agca face-to-face in intimate conversation. The pope had wisely excluded tape recorders from intruding on his conversation with his would-be killer. The two men talked in hushed tones. At the end of twenty-one minutes, both men were in tears. The assailant kissed the pope's ring and brushed the tears that were streaming down his unshaven face. He had been forgiven and spiritually absolved of his crime.

In a public statement made after the historic visit, the pope said, "Today, after two years, I am able to meet my assailant and repeat the pardon that I expressed from the hospital. Providence led things in their own way, I would say in an extraordinary and also wonderful way." He went on to say that it was

". . . a historic day in my life as a man, a Christian, as a bishop, and bishop of Rome."

The absolution did not change Agca's prison sentence. The pope had not intended that. What he had intended and accomplished was a fulfillment of Jesus' admonition to forgive our enemies and cleanse our memories of debilitating resentment.

While most of the world cheered this act of initiative forgiveness, some were outraged. How could the pope publicly forgive one convicted of murder in a previous case and now serving out a life sentence for an attempted assassination? Agca had been convicted of murdering Abdi Ipekci, a Turkish newspaper editor, in Istanbul. It was after escaping from jail that he took his next assignment as the pope's assassin. Yet the pontiff had called him a brother.

The Turkish daily *Milliyet* stirred other feelings in the world's heart. Feelings of justice and unforgiven wrongs, unconfessed and unabsolved. "What is shocking," a *Milliyet* spokesman said, "is the fact that the pope describes him as a brother and says he enjoys his complete trust. How can the pontiff treat as trustworthy a terrorist whose hands are still stained with Ipekci's blood?"

What the spokesman did not understand was that the "complete trust" the pope had referred to was the intimate openness of the confessional the spiritual leader had initiated. Obviously Agca had responded to that unqualified love and confessed his act of hateful terror against him. Then the pope mediated the power of absolution, a power of forgiveness entrusted by Christ to all Christians.

We may never know the full residual results of that forgiveness in the assassin's spiritual life. What we do know is that the pope had received and expressed the liberating power of the healing of the memory of a nearly fatal attempt on his life. It's one thing to feel the resistance of your opponents and the angry hatred of your enemies, but quite another to deal with the focused violence of one who wanted you dead. That's a gouging wound in any leader's psyche. And John Paul cherished his own peace of soul and deemed his future effectiveness as a spiritual leader too crucial to harbor hurting and unhealed memories. It was both Agca's and his own need that sent the pope to the prison to be a peacemaker.

Hurting and Unhealed Memories

The reason this event in the midst of the busy Christmas season of 1983 received so much attention by the media and by all of us was not just because of the notoriety of a pope who insists on speaking and acting on the truth as he sees it. The real reason we responded with awe and admiration was because we all have unhealed memories. Things people have said and done to us fester in our souls. We believe we are right, our judgments righteous, and our unwillingness to forgive the only way of punishing. What we know in our deepest hearts, however, is that our punishment through unexpressed forgiveness and a refusal to be initiative reconcilers is harming us more severely than the people who have wronged us.

Our inability to forgive others is usually related to our memories of our own failures. We all have those disturbing memories of things we've done and said that make us self-condemnatory. Often we are harder on ourselves than we are on other people.

The ability to remember is a divinely endowed gift. With this endowment we collect knowledge through study and experience. The memory bank in our brains contains all that has happened to and around us, as well as the data and information we have memorized. Our problem is that our facility to remember is not capable of selection. We hold on to good and bad memories with equal tenacity.

There's a humorous story about two men who were discussing their wives. One said that he loved his wife very much, but every time they got into an argument, she became historical. "You mean *hysterical,*" the other man replied. "No, *historical,*" the man asserted. "She keeps bringing up the past."

The point of the story applies to husbands as well as wives. It could have been told about two wives talking about their husbands or about two friends of either sex talking about people in their lives who remember hurting things stored in their memories. For all of us the *historical* can make us *hysterical* or irrational and incapable of grasping the potential of the future. What shall we do with the disturbing memories of what we have done or others have done to us?

The disturbing truth is that we cannot heal ourselves. Rehearsing the troublesome memories often makes them worse than they are. Talking them out with a friend or a trained counselor focuses their debilitating reality, but usually does not result in the ability to forget or forgive. The memories that hurt us must be taken to a higher court than our own perception and evaluation. Once we have dredged up the past, we need power greater than our own to deal with what really happened and then receive and mediate healing.

Christ, Healer of Memories

Only Christ, the healing power of the world, can heal the pain of the past. A crucial aspect of His healing in our lives is the healing of memories. Just as surely as His Spirit at work in our bodies is the source of physical healing, so, too, He can expunge from the tissues of the memory portion of the cerebral cortex the disturbing memories we have surrendered to Him.

The account of the healing of the woman caught in adultery recorded in John 8:1–11 helps us to understand and appropriate Christ's power to heal memories. The scribes and Pharisees used the woman to test Jesus. He used the unhealed memories in the Pharisees' minds to clear the way for the healing of the disturbing memories in the woman, which were keeping her from a new life. The difference is that the woman was healed, and the scribes and Pharisees were left to live with the exposed but unhealed scars of their own failures.

Remember how the Lord did it? The woman caught in the act of adultery was placed before Jesus by the scribes and Pharisees. "Teacher, this woman was caught in adultery, in the very act. Now Moses, in the law, commanded us that such should be stoned. But what do You say?" (vv. 4, 5) they said as they held their execution stones poised in their hands.

The concern was not the sin of the woman, but the desire to test and try Jesus. The religious leaders wanted data of an actual denial of the law of Moses by Jesus. If He forgave the woman or stayed her execution, they would have one more vital factor in the case they were seeking to build against Him.

Some brief background is helpful. The leaders wanted Jesus to give an interpretation of the Jewish law. The law of Moses clearly said that the woman's crime was punishable by stoning to death. However, the Romans had taken away from the Jews the right of inflicting the death penalty. If Jesus maintained the law of Moses, saying that the woman should be stoned, He would be charged with opposing Roman law. On the other hand, leniency about Moses would open Him to the charge that He lowered moral standards. The leaders thought they had Him in the tight vise of an impossible dilemma. Not so!

Jesus did not answer immediately. Instead He stooped down and wrote on the ground with His finger. There have been countless theories about what He wrote. Some say He simply made meaningless marks on the ground, while He gained control of His impatience with the leaders and had time to think through His response. Others have postulated that He wrote some of the Ten Commandments, which the scribes and Pharisees might have been equally guilty of breaking, in attitude if not in deed.

I have often thought that perhaps He wrote the Hebrew letters for *I AM, YAHWEH,* spoken twenty-three times in His self-declaration of His divine authority in such statements as, ". . . Before Abraham was, I AM," or ". . . I am the light of the world" (John 8:58; John 9:5). That would have asserted His authority over either the law of Moses or the Romans. Still others have reasoned that what Jesus wrote on the ground was what He subsequently spoke when the leaders pressed Him for an answer. The point is, we do not know. Whatever it was prepared the way for the scribes and Pharisees to feel the full impact of what He said.

Rising to His full height, Jesus looked the accusers squarely in the eyes and said, "He who is without sin among you, let him throw a stone at her first" (v. 7). In so speaking, He denied neither Mosaic nor Roman law. He was not abolishing moral requirements or approving denial of Roman authority. He rose above both by piercing the memories of past sin in the leaders' own lives. How the Lord said His convicting words must have been as powerful as what He said. Imagine the intensity with which He spoke.

The word used to translate the two words "without sin" is one word in the Greek. It means complete freedom from sin in nature, character, and experience. Only Christ Himself could make that claim. In substance He was saying, "Only one who is sinless has the right to exact the penalty—only God and His Messiah have that qualification." The leaders were shocked.

Suddenly from the memory bank of their own minds leaped

the guilt over past sins, if not in the area of adultery, certainly in other infractions of God's law. But none of them either rose to their own defense or made confession of their sins. One by one, beginning with the oldest, they dropped their stones and crept away. In the presence of the power exuding from Jesus, they had been confronted with reality. That confrontation always demands a decision, a retreat, or repentance. None had the courage to do the last.

When all the scribes and Pharisees had left, Jesus turned the full attention of His love and forgiveness upon the woman. He forced her to see that all her accusers were gone. "Woman," He said, "where are those accusers of yours? Has no one condemned you?" Looking about in amazement she said, "No one, Lord." Then with divine authority, the sinless One who was greater than Moses and had more power than all the legions of Rome gave her the healing absolution she desperately needed: "Neither do I condemn you; go and sin no more" (vv. 10, 11).

We hear those same words spoken to us from this side of Calvary. The sinless One took our sins and atoned for them in a once, never-to-be-repeated substitutionary sacrifice for us. Through Him we are justified, declared "not guilty!"

Forgiven, Cleansed, Healed

Now the computers of our minds can be cleared of all the memories we harbor of our failures, mistakes, and inadequacies in the past. Those memories, if not forgiven and cleansed, fester in us. Some are so painful they are pressed down into the subconscious, yet signal the conscious mind with disturbing thoughts of guilt, fear, tension, and anxiety. Eventually they congeal into an overall attitude of self-condemnation or dread. We may believe in Jesus Christ but still carry the heavy burden of hurting memories of our failures and the distressing things people have done or said to us in the past. Only a profound experience of Christ's forgiveness in us, and then through us to others, can set us free. We need to hear and appropriate Christ's words, "Neither do I condemn you." Then we need to say that to ourselves. Finally we need to say it to people who have hurt us.

One way to do that, which I have found very helpful, is through a prayer therapy. Give yourself the gift of several unencumbered, interruption-free hours. Get off by yourself in comfortable surroundings where you can be quiet.

Open the time of prayerful reflection by affirming that the Lord is present, that you belong to Him, and that He loves you unreservedly. Think about His atoning death for you. Reflect on His forgiveness, freely offered to you. Repeat these words, "I am forgiven. My confession is not to be forgiven, but because I am already. I believe it and accept it as a basic fact of my life."

Now take a pen and paper. Ask the Lord to guide your mind to any memories that are distressing you. Let your mind drift freely back over the years. Write each painful memory carefully. This is your private time with the Lord; don't be afraid to let the memories flow. What causes you to feel guilty, hurt, anxious? Put down both what you've done and what others have done to you. Don't evaluate them yet. Just write what comes to mind.

When the flow of memories subsides, you are ready to go back over the list to pray about each one specifically. Then articulate to the Lord your perception of what you did or what happened to you. Ask the Lord for the forgiveness He's already provided through Calvary. Then thank Him for *your* forgiveness and total absolution. In each case of the memory of your own failure, whatever it was, say your own name and announce to yourself that since Christ does not condemn you, you will no longer condemn yourself. When the memories involve what other people have said or done, picture the person in your mind's eye and say his or her name, along with words of forgiveness.

The Lord will guide the whole process. His healing Spirit will wipe out the anguish, guilt, and judgment you feel toward yourself and the resentment you feel toward others. It can and will happen!

Restitution and Confession

There are times when restitution must be coupled with confession, when the memory involves things we have said or done to hurt people. This must be done under the guidance of the Spirit of Christ. Tell Him you are ready and willing. Then if He brings it back to your mind, be sure to act on His guidance.

When you go to another person to seek forgiveness, don't rehearse the whole situation in detail. Simply refer to the failure and express your sorrow for what you did or said and ask for forgiveness. The success of the encounter is not in whether the person is able to say he or she forgives you. You are responsible for your willingness to make restitution, not the other person's reaction.

In the same way, the Lord must guide your expression of forgiveness to people. Never use the expression of forgiveness as an opportunity to remind people of how much they have hurt or troubled you. That's further guilt-producing incrimination. Just assure them of your love and your forgiveness. Then follow that up with affirmation and reassurance in word and action. The sure test of whether we have really forgiven someone is if we act as if the person had not said or done the things that prompted the need for forgiveness.

This quality of prayer therapy and restitution must be practiced often. We tend to gather up hurting memories and need to unload them on a consistent basis. The Lord is always ready to help us. In fact He motivates the desire in us. He created us and wants to recreate us.

Memories and Physical Health

Our spiritual, emotional, and physical health are dependent on the consistent healing of memories. The memory is part of our thinking brain, in technical terms called the cerebral cortex. It is responsible for our intellectual functions, including thinking, imagining, fantasizing, dreaming, and talking, as well as memory. The cerebral cortex is closely related to the limbic system, which controls our emotions, heartbeat, and breathing as well as the input of hormones into the bloodstream through the hypothalamus, pituitary, and endocrine glands. The limbic system gets its signals from the cerebral cortex.

What we think affects our total nervous system and body functions. When we are troubled, anxious, or under stress, alarm signals are sent, arousing the limbic system's emotional and physiological responses. When we are under inordinate or consistently recurring stress, we keep our system in an agitated state of arousal. One of the results of this is that the limbic system pumps chemicals called catecholamines into the bloodstream. These cause high cholesterol, the overproduction of clotting platelets, and a possible clogging of the veins and arteries. In this highly agitated state, our body's immune system is debilitated, making us more susceptible to disease.

Unhealed memories contribute to a constant state of alarm from the cerebral cortex to the limbic system. The same thoughts are repeated, producing the same response as if the circumstance of the memory was actually happening now. Pile up the bad memories, and our bodies will remain in a state of high anxiety. When we couple memory with the imagination, we actually relive the hurting memory, and our emotions and body responses react accordingly.[1]

Now we can appreciate how crucial is the healing of our memories. Often they must be healed before the body can function properly to ward off physical problems. Prayer for physical healing must include the healing of the memory, if the total nervous system is to be a channel of Christ's healing power. Nursing troublesome memories is like taking a constant dose of poison. It is a sign of lack of love for ourselves, a refusal to accept Christ's love and forgiveness.

Each week, when people are invited to come forward to the chancel to pray with the elders of our congregation for the healing of their spiritual, physical, and emotional needs, I include the healing of memories in my invitation. Bad memories need to be cured before they lodge destructively in negative thought patterns of self-condemnation or judgment of others. Many people who for years have suffered from self-incriminating memories have come with needs and been healed. Others with long-standing resentments against others have been released to forgive and forget. Often the time of prayer is followed with counseling by the elders. In cases where the person needs prolonged help as a part of Christ's healing, he or she is referred to one of the Christian psychologists in our Creative Counseling Center.

Recently a visitor to our services responded to the Sunday-morning invitation for prayer for healing. He told the elder he had suffered with a dull ache in his chest for months. He had been to his doctor and had a thorough checkup. The physician had told him that his problem was stress and that he needed to slow down. What he had not told his doctor was that he was filled with resentment toward his wife, who had left him. Now he must raise three teenage children alone.

That morning the message had been on forgiveness. The Lord put His finger on the resentment in the man and revealed to him that it was the cause of the emotional, but very real, ache in his chest. When he came to the chancel for prayer, the elder, guided by the Spirit, simply asked, "Are there any memories that need to be healed?" The man was astounded by the discernment the elder displayed. Briefly he unburdened the resentment that was eating him alive. As the elder prayed the ache in the man's chest lessened and by the end of the prayer was lifted completely.

Keeping in touch with the man for weeks afterward, the elder learned that the prayer of healing was the beginning of a new life for him. He began to take time each day for prayer and soon became part of a support group that meets weekly for Bible study and prayer. His own words explain his healing. "That time for prayers of healing that Sunday saved my life! It's amazing—all through those anguishing times with my wife and the disappointment of the divorce, I felt I was right and that my resentment was justified indignation. Then the memory of it all haunted me and the anger grew like a malignancy in my soul. Funny thing—I was a Christian all that time and couldn't forgive my wife. Now that I have, I can begin living again."

Set Free From the Past

The power of Christ to heal memories and set people free from the past is further exemplified in what He did for a couple in our congregation. I've been given permission to tell this story. The couple involved wants it known. What happened to them, they yearn to have happen to other couples. Their very exciting healing occurred as a result of experiencing the power of forgiveness.

I remember when I first heard about them. Their physician called me. He said that he and the psychiatrist needed my help. The husband was in the hospital, very ill with stomach difficulties, a very serious case of ulcers. His stomach was being eaten out as a result of the worry. The doctor said, "We need to get together. As we understand it, the real problem is that this man's wife will not forgive him of an infraction of their marital vows. As a result, she feels that she must judge him and keep him at arm's length."

The five of us—the internist and the psychiatrist, the couple, and I—gathered together. We talked over the situation. I realized that deeper counseling was going to be necessary for the wife. She felt so righteous in her indignation. She had taken vengeance into her own hands and felt called to punish her husband for what he had done. Her attitude toward him was aloof, cold, and negative. As a result she allowed no affection between them and constantly reminded him of what he had done to hurt her. His appeals for forgiveness and a new chance were rejected. At the same time she did not believe in divorce and was determined to live the rest of her life with the sword of hostility drawn.

Later, after a long time of listening and caring as the wife and I talked alone, I said, "Dear friend, have you ever failed in your own sexual life?" Her face drained of blood. She became white. She said, "Why did you ask that question? You have no right to ask that question! What does that have to do with my inability to forgive my husband?" Persisting, I said, "Just tell me. Was there ever a time when you failed, either in attitude or in action?"

Then, tumbling out of her heart, came the story of a failure in her teenage years, with an older man, and all the problems that had resulted. She'd covered it up. Thought no one knew. Kept it from her parents and her friends, the memory guarded deep down inside her. Her unforgiving memory had caused her to deal with her husband's failure with such terrible indignation and vengeance.

The woman seemed relieved that at least one person knew about her secret. When she felt reassured of my confidentiality, she talked about it freely, relating the guilt and anguish the memory had caused her.

When the timing was right, I asked, "Could it be that your guilt over what you have done has made it especially difficult to forgive your husband? Is there an interrelationship between your inability to accept forgiveness and forgive yourself, and your refusal to forgive your husband?"

As we talked further she realized that her husband's failure had forced her to relive her own. What she had been doing to him she really felt she had deserved. Yet since no one knew, she had felt she was left to be her own judge. Her childhood conditioning in the Christian faith had been focused on rules and regulations. There had been little or no teaching or experience in forgiveness. And what she had done was, in her mind, the one thing God would never forgive. She had suppressed her feelings all through the years. Then, when she learned of her husband's mistake, she let them fly with vengeance.

I shared with this distraught wife the truth of Scripture about Christ's forgiveness and unconditional love. Then we talked about His power to heal memories. The Lord blessed the conversation, creating a willingness in the woman to let go of her false idea about His condemnation and releasing her to consider the truth of His compassion. Her reverence for the Bible was a dynamic plus. We went through passage after passage about grace. Finally she was ready to surrender her hurting memory for Christ's healing. We prayed together, accepting the Lord's forgiveness for her.

In a subsequent visit, we focused on the implications of her healed memory for her forgiveness for her husband. She related how <u>her feelings about him had mysteriously changed</u> <u>since she felt healed of the past.</u> A new tenderness and warmth began to grow in her. We talked through how she could communicate forgiveness to her husband in words, actions, and attitudes. She pictured the actual way and words that she would use. Again we prayed. Then she left my office to go to the hospital to be a channel of Christ's love for her husband. It worked. She told him about her own experience of healing and expressed tender forgiveness.

In the weeks that followed, the husband began to recover. He responded readily to treatment and soon was able to go home. Nourished by the new relationship between him and his wife, he was able to return to work long before the doctors had expected.

The man's experience of his wife's forgiveness was only the beginning of a spiritual pilgrimage still ahead of him. He still needed to accept the Lord's forgiveness. I saw him in church each week, listening intently. Then one Sunday my heart leaped with joy as I saw him come down the aisle and pray with one of the elders. He claimed the Lord's forgiveness for his failure and asked for the healing of his memory.

Some weeks later both the husband and wife came forward for prayer. Afterward they exclaimed, "That was more than a healing service at the end of this morning's service. For us it was a remarriage service!" And so it was. Christ, the healing power of the world, had healed their individual memories and had made them one again. His words sounded in my soul as I looked into their radiant faces, "Neither do I condemn you. . . ." Then my heart sang with Paul's words, "There is therefore now no condemnation to those who are in Christ Jesus . . ." (Romans 8:1).

And so it happens. Christ is the healer of memories for the pope or for any of us. We are prompted to ask, "What memories does He long to heal in me?" Tell Him all about it. Then He will help you receive what has been yours all along: forgiveness and the power to forgive.

8 Is Sickness Caused by Sin?

Mark Twain once said that a classic is a book everyone knows about and nobody ever reads. I want to suggest that a classic question is one everybody asks and few attempt to answer.

One of the most troublesome classic questions that's been around for centuries and is being asked more frequently today is: "Is sickness caused by sin?" When people pray for themselves or others intercede for them and they continue to be ill, the implication is that there may be some hidden sin or unhealed memory in the past that is blocking the Lord's healing power.

I hear people ask this question about themselves in many different ways. A man I visited recently, who had had a crippling stroke, asked, "Lloyd, what did I do to deserve this? I must have really sinned for God to have done this to me!"

129

A woman who has endured a long illness confided the same concern with tears in her eyes. "I've prayed, and the Lord just doesn't seem to hear. There must be something wrong with me or the way I've been praying, that I've not been healed. I keep searching for what it might be. I lie awake at night, trying to think what it might be. I've confessed and reconfessed every mistake or failure of my life that I can recall, and still I don't get well. What more can I possibly do to deserve the Lord's healing?"

A man stricken with disease put the same fear in another way. He explained, "I know I've drifted away from the Lord. I used to be a faithful believer when I was a kid, but over the years I've not taken time to think much about God or to pray. If He gave me this sickness to get my attention, well, He's certainly got it! But now that I am praying again, I still don't get well. What's wrong with me?"

Another person put it bluntly. "I must have been a terrible sinner for this sickness to have happened to me!"

Equally distressing are the questions raised by friends and loved ones when a person does not get well. There's an idea held by many Christians today that sickness is caused by sin, and when their prayers for a person are not answered when and how they want, some explanation must be offered. Often it is that some guilt over something in the past or some resentful attitude in the present is keeping the person from experiencing healing. These critics and pious analysts keep the almighty word *always* at the top of their healing lexicon. God *always* heals the sick, they imply, and if healing doesn't happen, the sick person must be to blame. Added to the sickness a person is suffering is the load of self-incrimination piled upon himself or herself as a result of the judgments of others.

A young woman I talked to the other day is an example of this. In her efforts to get well, she's had one disappointment after another. She called me to talk about an alarming visit she had had from a group of her friends. Out of concern for her prolonged illness, they had sought the advice of a spiritual healer in their community. After hearing the details of the case, he suggested that the friends confront the woman about the possibility of some unconfessed sin in her life. When they did that, the suffering woman was crushed. The attitude of judgment created an atmosphere in which she could not have talked out any spiritual problem, if she had had one.

The Great Physician Speaks

All these illustrations of simplistic answers to the question "Is sickness caused by sin?" have tended to distract us from finding a more profound answer. We must push aside all the pros and cons and look to the Great Physician for an answer. Then, based on what He said, we will draw some helpful conclusions for our life today.

In John 9 the man born blind prompted the disciples to ask this same question in slightly different words. Jesus' answer becomes a foundation stone on which to build an understanding of the relationship between sin and sickness.

One day, after Jesus finished a heated confrontation with the Jewish leaders in the temple, He paused to observe a man who had been blind from birth. I sense He looked with empathy and compassion, discerning what He might do for him. The disciples were interested in the Master's concern about the man. Obviously they knew about the man and probably had talked often about the cause of his blindness. If the man had been blind from birth, who had sinned? They were happy to be able to receive the Master's wisdom about this man. "Rabbi, who sinned, this man or his parents, that he was born blind?" they asked urgently (v. 2).

The way they asked leaves little doubt about how they would answer the question we are posing in this chapter. Obviously they held the belief current at that time that sickness was indeed caused by sin.

But whose sin? The man's? If so he must have sinned prior to birth, because he was born blind. Perhaps they entertained that possibility because of another idea popular at that time. Many believed that original sin entered into an unborn child while he was still in the mother's womb. Therefore, many thought, a child was born in a state of sin. Or did the disciples believe in some form of reincarnation? Did they reason that the soul of someone who had lived previously had entered into the man before he was born? If so, they may have reasoned that the sin of the reincarnated soul was the cause of the blindness. Any of these beliefs might have been the basis of the strange suggestion that the man himself was the cause of his own blindness.

And what about the parents? Could some sin in their lives have been the cause? Had they sinned prior to marriage, had they been unfaithful to each other and broken God's laws, or had they contracted some kind of disease that infected the mother's body, thus contaminating the child's eyes and causing the blindness? Behind that line of reasoning would have been the idea that God would punish the parents for their sin by making the child blind.

Jesus brushed aside the possibility of sin either in the parents or the man as the cause of his blindness. His answer, however, needs careful study. In the New King James Bible it is stated as follows:

Neither this man nor his parents sinned, but that the works of God should be revealed in him. I must work the works of Him who sent Me while it is day; the night

is coming when no one can work. As long as I am in
the world, I am the light of the world.

John 9:3–5

Now it's very important how these verses are punctuated.
The meaning is radically affected by where the commas and
periods are placed. As you know, the Greek original manuscripts of the New Testament had no punctuation. That was
left to later translators. We do not give the same kind of divine
authority to the punctuation marks as we do to the original
writers of the Scriptures, who wrote under the inspired guidance of the Holy Spirit.

Since none of us were there to hear Jesus speak this crucial
statement about sin, sickness, and His messianic calling as the
Light of the World, we must consider carefully what He meant
and how the punctuation is placed. With all due respect to the
translators of our contemporary versions of the Bible, I think
the punctuation of some versions leads us to the wrong conclusion about what Jesus really intended in these momentous
verses.

Look at them again as they stand in most translations. "Neither this man nor his parents sinned, but that the works of God
should be revealed in him. I must work the works of Him who
sent Me while it is day; the night is coming when no one can
work. As long as I am in the world, I am the light of the
world."

Reading it that way suggests that this blind man was set up
as a ploy on the stage of history, so that Jesus could reveal His
healing power. In other words, God made the man blind and
kept him that way for some thirty years, until Christ came and
the appointed time for the healing miracle arrived. Do we believe in a God like that? We know that God is in ultimate control of all things, and nothing happens that He does not allow.

But can we go further to say that He made the man blind so that Jesus could do the works He sent Him to do?

Now let's take that same passage and punctuate it differently. "Neither this man nor his parents sinned. But that the works of God should be revealed in Him, I must work the works of Him who sent me while it is day; the night is coming when no one can work. As long as I am in the world, I am the light of the world." This punctuation established more clearly what my study and prayer reveals Jesus meant. He did not blame the parents or the son. The important issue was to do the works of God in the man and heal him. He could do that because of His I AM authority as Immanuel, God with us.

In many instances, Jesus identified physical and psychological sickness as the work of Satan and evil spirits. In this case He chose to place the emphasis on the power of God to heal through Him. When He did heal the blind man, He simply spat on the ground and made clay with the saliva and anointed the man's eyes with the clay. It was the touch of the Master's hand that eventually made the man see, when—at the Lord's command—he went to the Pool of Siloam to wash his eyes of the clay.

The liberating good news for you and me is that the Lord is with us today to heal all of our needs. He is the Light of the World, working still. He does not make us sick so that by healing us He can be glorified. He loves us too much for that. Nor does He send sickness as a punishment for our sins. He is with us to forgive us our sins and to release His healing power for our illnesses and troubles.

Two Answers: Yes and No

In that light, we can confront the question with which we began this chapter. Is sickness caused by sin? In answering, I am reminded of a professor friend of mine who often answers profound questions by saying, "Well, yes and no." Then he gives the truth of both the yes and the no. Our question demands that kind of response.

Yes, sickness in general is caused by sin. We live in a fallen creation. Humankind's sin has distorted God's plan for the world. His original intention for our health, harmony, and well-being has been disordered by our rebellion. Therefore, as a part of this fallen world there are diseases, germs, and sickness.

Through Adam's sin and centuries of humankind's rebellion and hostility against God, we are susceptible to pain and disability. Paul puts this clearly in Romans 5:12, 14.

> Therefore, just as through one man sin entered the world, and death through sin, and thus death spread to all men, because all sinned. . . . Nevertheless death reigned from Adam to Moses, even over those who had not sinned according to the likeness of the transgression of Adam, who is a type of Him who was to come.

That's the grim diagnosis of human history. But God did not leave us there. He sent Christ to be a new Adam, the beginning of a new creation.

> For if by the one man's offense death reigned through the one, much more those who receive abundance of grace and of the gift of righteousness will reign in life through the One, Jesus Christ. Therefore, as through one man's offense judgment came to all men, resulting in condemnation, even so through one Man's righteous act the free gift came to all men, resulting in justification of life. For as by one man's dis-

obedience many were made sinners, so also by one
Man's obedience many will be made righteous.

Romans 5:17–19

Further, *yes, some sickness in particular is caused by sin.* Remember the basic meaning of sin as separation from God,
missing the mark, and willfully seeking to run our own lives.
Sin is not just what we do wrong, but what we become when
we are not in fellowship with God and under the guidance of
His Spirit. That separation makes us vulnerable to distorted
thinking, confused emotions, and inordinate tension in our
bodies.

The more we study some types of sickness, the more we see
how closely related illness can be to our thinking and reactions.
In our society, which is guided by law, moral standards of right
and wrong, and varying degrees of ethical behavior, many
people fail. But without any relationship with the Lord, they
have no way in which that guilt can be resolved.

Still others have inherited Christian moral principles without the Lord's power to fulfill them or His grace when they
blunder and fall. Often unresolved guilt is the source of physical disorders. Unhealed memories, attitudes of anger and resentment, and persistent misuse of our bodies will cause
sickness. These things and others like them too numerous to
list are the result of the sins of either not wanting the Lord or a
refusal to live in His abundant grace.

Finally, *yes, sickness is sometimes caused by the sinful attitudes of those around us.* How we relate to people who are ill
greatly affects their recovery. I remember well an experience of
praying for a young man whose parents had given up hope that
he would get well. Every time I prayed in their presence I felt
the impact of their despair. But there was something more. The
husband and wife were not happy with each other. Their marriage had been very stormy right from the beginning.

Years before, they had decided to separate. Then, in a last effort to try to work at the marriage, they had agreed to give life together one more try. During that period of brief reconciliation, their son had been conceived. When he was born, the couple decided they would have to stay together to raise him.

Now, seventeen years later, their relationship was more stormy than ever. They were very angry with each other and subliminally with their son. He had been the only reason they had endured each other. Through the years, the boy had not felt consistent love and encouragement. The parents had vacillated between harsh discipline and solicitous permissiveness. Often he had been the brunt of their hostility toward each other. The result was that he searched for love and attention in other ways. In the last couple of years, he was constantly in trouble at school and in the community. An accident with the family car had injured him seriously. The surgeons and physicians had done everything they could to save him. Yet he was not responding. Something was wrong inside both him and his parents.

The young man had lost the will to live. At the time the doctors needed him to fight for his life as vigorously as they were, he was not responding. When his parents visited him, he got worse. For a time, I had to ask them to leave the room when I prayed for his healing. The static created by the turbulent family relationships had become counterproductive to healing.

As the young man became strong enough to speak I had to talk out with him his feelings about his parents. He had to be released from the false idea that he was the cause or could be the cure of his parents' marital difficulties. Then he needed a reason to get well. That required new self-esteem and some specific hopes and dreams for his future. Eventually he began to talk about his suppressed longing to go on to college and study engineering. Finally we were able to talk about his relationship to the Lord.

Attendance at Sunday school and participation in the youth groups had given the young man a belief in Christ, but he had never accepted His love for him and had not made a commitment of his life to Him. After several conversations about the Lord's power to help him get well and guide his future, the young man turned his life over to Christ. From that point on his will to live was strengthened, and by cooperating with the Lord's healing power, he began to get well.

I'm thankful to say that he graduated with his high-school class and now is well along in his college career. Most important of all, the Lord has freed him from the tangled web of his parents' ambivalence. He's on his own, yet not really—he's alive in Christ and dependent on His strength and courage as he is earning his way through college and looking forward to what the future holds.

I wish I could say that this healing brought the parents to Christ and to a new life together. When the young man has tried to share his faith, they have been very resistant. I suspect that inwardly they know that if they accept Christ's love, they'll have to face the need to love each other. In the meantime they are muddling in the midst of unresolved tensions. They refuse to be whole. The sickness in their marriage is, indeed, caused by that sin of resistance.

The Other Side of the Ledger

Now, let's look on the "no" side of the ledger in response to the question, "Is sickness caused by sin?"

No, the Lord does not punish us with sickness as a retribution for our sin. He loves us too much for that. He is in the battle with us, seeking to release His healing power for all our needs.

He is for us and not against us. Once we accept that awesome fact, we can greet Him as our Friend, not as an enemy or an angry, hostile judge.

The people whose stories I told at the opening of this chapter were suffering from both their physical difficulties and an untruth. When sickness struck, they immediately thought they were to blame. That set up further impediments to receiving the Lord's healing power. Blaming ourselves or others is simply another block placed in our path. We end up blaming God, who we think sent the sickness to bring us into line.

The most important thing is to be in an open, receptive relationship with the Lord. If we suspect that something in our life-style, unhealed memories, attitudes, or relationships might have made us vulnerable to becoming sick or not getting well, then let's confess it and clear the channels for receiving the Lord's help. Self-incrimination is really playing God. It's a substitute for confession. Confession opens us up to receive grace and deep inner peace.

In our efforts to be communicators of the Lord's love to others who are ill, our task is not to accuse or level judgments. Profound caring alone will provide an ambience in which people can talk out anything that may be rankling in their souls. I find that words like these are helpful, "I'm praying for you. The Lord loves you very much. He is the healing power of the world. He's here with you and is at work in you. Trust Him completely. Are there any worries or troublesome things on your mind? Let's give them to the Lord so that you can be free to relax and receive His grace. Before I pray with you, is there anything you want to talk about?"

Notice that I didn't use the word *sin.* For most patients it's a guilt-producing word that raises their defenses. By far the best way to help a person who is suffering is to listen. Profound empathy will draw to the surface anything that needs to be shared. The more sensitive and caring we are, the more a person will be able to confide feelings pent up inside.

Come Cry With Me

I am reminded of one of the crucial turning points in my wife Mary Jane's healing from cancer. She had fought the battle valiantly. Through it all she had prayed, and we'd prayed together. At times the progress was disappointing. All through the ordeal, Mary Jane had not allowed her feelings to surface in tears. If one of her loved ones or friends had gone through what she had, she would have readily expressed her sympathy and love with tears. But she had not allowed herself to cry over what had been happening.

One day our good friend and fellow adventurer in Christ, Dr. John Stehlin of Houston, Texas, the world-famous cancer surgeon and specialist, made a special trip up to Los Angeles to see her. He reviewed all the charts and prognoses and gave some medical insight from his immense knowledge and skill. But the main thing he did was to encourage Mary Jane to cry. He sensed the pent-up emotions and the need for release.

A couple of years later John was back in Los Angeles for a rest. He was exhausted from months of operations and care for sick and dying people. He needed assurance that the Lord really cared and was there with him on what he calls the "front-line trenches of human suffering."

After a long visit, I felt led to give him the gift he had given Mary Jane. "John, I think you want to cry, don't you?" He did and then returned to his clinic in Houston to join the Lord in His healing ministry.

I told that story one night in Washington, D.C., at a convention. Joyce Landorf, the famous author and speaker, was there. At the time she was enduring excruciating pain in her jaw. The account of Mary Jane's release, and subsequently John's, touched her deeply. Later that night, in her hotel room, she penned this poem.

Come Cry With Me
You came along and said hello.
    You asked, "How are you today?"
I almost answered, "I'm just fine,"
    as is my usual way.
But something in your eyes and face
    said, "That's not a greeting! I really care."
It freed me to open up, to speak my mind,
    to really share.
"You see I may look well and whole,
    but inside I'm a bruised and a broken soul.
I struggle with the loneliness of pain.
    And I do ask why,
But mostly I hurt, long to be hugged,
    and desperately want to cry."
You looked at me for just a moment
    then opened up your arms and said—
    "Come cry with me,
Let it all flow out like rivers toward the sea.
    Come cry with me,
Let me hold you now. For wherever wounded spirits
    gather together, there's the Lord, there's you and
    there's me.
    Come cry with me."

Satan: The Real Enemy

The next thing I want to say as a part of the "no" side of the truth in search for our answer to the question "Is sickness caused by sin?" is to take a careful look at the word *caused*. That word implies the primary source. *The cause of sickness is Satan and his destructive, life-debilitating influence in the world.* He would be delighted to have us think that our sin was the primary cause of sickness. That takes the focus off him and puts it on us. He uses our difficulties to try to influence our thinking. He wants us to blame ourselves, other people, even God. Most of all he seeks to keep us from trusting the Lord completely. His efforts are to drive a wedge between us and the Lord. Since, from the Lord's point of view, there is nothing that will make Him stop loving us, the only recourse Satan has is to make us think the Lord doesn't care or has forgotten us. Satan is the source of doubting questions that lead to discouragement.

In these times, we need to understand our real enemy and rediscover the power entrusted to us to confront him straight on. We have been given the powerful name of Jesus Christ and a full suit of armor for our prayers against satanic influence. Christ is more powerful than any evil force in the world. During His incarnation, the Lord confronted Satan, evil spirits, and demons. At His commanding word they were rendered impotent. He went to the cross to defeat the power of Satan. The cross was the breaking of the stranglehold of evil on the world. Now through His living presence He entrusts that same victorious power to us.

The two things that overcome evil influence are the cross and the name of Jesus Christ. When we reclaim our status and security through the cross and pray in the name of Jesus Christ, we are surrounded by the Lord's protective, shielding spirit and freed from the hassling of evil influence.

Satan's tactic is to put us on the defensive with self-doubt and self-condemnation. Christ calls us to take the offensive. That's what He meant when He told Peter and the disciples that the gates of hades could not prevail against the power He would give them.

After Peter was given the gift of the Spirit to believe in Jesus as the Christ, the Lord said, "Blessed are you, Simon Bar-Jonah, for flesh and blood has not revealed this to you, but My Father who is in heaven. And I also say to you that you are Peter, and on this rock I will build My church, and the gates of Hades shall not prevail against it" (Matthew 16:17, 18). Look carefully at this promise. It is for us today as much as it was for Peter and the disciples or subsequently the early church.

An Indestructible Rock of Faith

The Spirit of God gave Peter the gift of faith to say to Jesus, "You are the Christ, the Son of the living God" (v. 16). Jesus' affirmation of that gift was coupled with an explanation of how it would be used. He would build His church on the rock of that dynamic, indestructible faith. It was Peter's faith, not the disciple himself, on which the church would be built. That same quality of faith would later be given to the others. With that faith, Christ's followers would be able to storm the gates of hades.

We need to take a careful look at the words *gates* and *hades*. The word *gates* meant "government." That idea came from the practice of the elders of a city meeting at the gate of the city to govern the affairs of the city and serve as a court of justice. The word *hades* meant the place of departed spirits and also became a synonym for death and the emanating source of evil. Now, what Jesus meant by *gates of hades* is the collusive, organized, destructive forces of evil. Now note that this unified force of evil would not be able to withstand the faith of the church. The gates of hades would not be able to withstand the power of Christ-filled men and women who were entrusted with the weapon of the name of Christ. We are not to be on the defensive, but the offensive, in an attack on evil.

In this battle we are encouraged by the fact that after Christ died on the cross He went to minister to the spirits in the prison of hades. The Apostles' Creed puts it, "He descended into hell." There He broke the power of the government (gates) of evil. So when we pray in His name and claim our status as belonging to Christ through the cross, Satan and his evil influence are banished.

Therefore, when negative, discouraged, and evil thoughts invade our minds and trouble or sickness distresses us, we can say, "Satan, you have no power over me. You were defeated by my Lord Christ, and now in His name, begone!" The one thing with which evil cannot coexist is the presence and power of Christ.

Focus on Christ—Claim Christ's Victory

Our great concern is to focus on Christ and not evil. The more we allow the Lord to fill us with Himself, the more powerful we become in facing the trials of life. We are not helpless victims.

Nor are we powerless in our ministry to one another in times of need. After Jesus had declared the power of faith over the government of evil, He said, "And I will give you the keys of the kingdom of heaven, and whatever you bind on earth will be bound in heaven, and whatever you loose on earth will be loosed in heaven" (Matthew 16:19). That awesome challenge tells us that we can bind Satan and loose people from their bonds of fear, doubt, unbelief, and crippling limitations. ⚡ ꜱꜱ

So often it's just the opposite. We bind people up with our negative judgments, attitudes, and actions. In so doing we loose Satan to influence them. The same is true of families, schedules, and the groups of which we are a part. What we say and how we act can debilitate prayers and frustrate growth. Instead, we are to claim our ministry of loosing people and groups. We are to do that by binding Satan in the name of Jesus. The same power Jesus exercised in liberating people during His ministry on earth is given to us. So let's claim Christ's victory!

The ministry of loosing people includes listening, loving, and liberating prayer in Christ's powerful name. In our private prayers about those who are sick, we should dare to say, "Christ, You are all-powerful. You are more powerful than evil, sickness, or the demons of doubt and discouragement. In Your name I ask You to bind Satan and loose this person." A version of that prayer can be prayed in the sick person's presence after we've talked with him or her about Christ's supremacy over all.

All the *yes*es and *no*es I've discussed in answer to the question, "Is sickness caused by sin?" fall short of helping us unless they bring us to a ministry of unbinding people with courageous prayer. Don't allow that question to trip you up in theological or psychological debate inside yourself or with others. Times of sickness create a great need for Christ, and our strength is in the fact that we have a great Christ for these needs. When the question does disturb us, we need to go to Him. And based on His response to the disciples about the cause of the man's blindness, hear Him say to us, "The important thing is not whether or not sickness is caused by sin, but that I, your forgiveness, healing, peace, and power, am with you."

9 Take My Hand, Lord!

Recently, while skiing in Colorado, I rode up the ski lift with another aspiring skier. We introduced ourselves and fell into a lively conversation about our efforts to learn how to ski with greater freedom from fear of falling. I confided that my skis often felt like the wheels of a Mack truck. My efforts to ski well with rhythm and ease frequently only reflected my lack of practice and limited time spent enjoying the sport.

My new friend responded by telling me some of the difficulties he was having getting his right leg to cooperate as a part of his coordinated body. He said, "You know, it's really ludicrous for us to think we can come out here once or twice a year and ski like experts. I guess we're just a couple of handicapped old men!"

Just then as the ski lift was nearing the top of the mountain we both looked down and saw a magnificent skier gliding down the mountain, with perfect skill and rhythm. Looking more closely, to our utter astonishment, the man had only one leg! To compensate for his missing leg, the man held a pole on which a little ski was attached. With the small ski at the end of the pole held in his hand and the regular-sized ski on his good leg, the man was skiing better than I ever hope to and better than most of the champions I've observed. My lift partner and I were amazed at the speed and ease with which the man streaked over the snow.

By this time we were at the top of the mountain, and it was time to prepare to get off and ski down the ramp in preparation for making our way down the mountain. Just as my new friend left the chair, he looked at me and winked with a smile, saying, "Good luck with your handicap!" What we had called our handicaps as novice skiers were nothing in comparison with what the one-legged skier had overcome.

Handicap: Word of Many Meanings

The word *handicap* comes from an old lottery practice that was called "hand in cap." The lottery tickets were drawn from a cap, but the winner was penalized. From that practice the idea of a handicap came to be used for a weight or impediment put on someone in an athletic contest who had advanced skill. It was used to balance off the odds.

In the case of foot races, the handicap was to hold back the most proficient and make him begin after the start signal was sounded. Today a handicap race of horses is when a horse that has had a winning streak is actually weighted down to even the others horses' potential to win.

The athletic use of the meaning of this word was pointed out to me recently when I was playing golf. On the first tee the friend with whom I was playing asked, "Lloyd, what's your handicap?" I laughed and said, "Well, I move my head, my stance is incorrect, and my swing is lousy!" My friend said, "I didn't ask you for excuses—what's your handicap?" In golf, a handicap is established on the basis of previous scores. A high-scoring golfer has a high handicap, while a more proficient, skilled golfer usually has a low handicap. The high handicap-per is given an advantage in the recording of the competitive scores.

Through the years, the word *handicap* has taken on a very different meaning. It has also come to mean whatever is a limiting physical, emotional, or intellectual disability that keeps us from functioning at full potential.

Every one of us has some kind of handicap. Something in our training or background limits our performance in life. Then there are those who have, most often through no fault of their own, challenging physical limitations. When I observe how efficiently many people with physical handicaps handle life, I wonder if some who seemingly have no obvious handicap may be the less fortunate because of the way they underuse their potential. As Helen Keller once said, "What could be worse than being blind? Having two good eyes and not be able to see the wonder all around them. I thank God for my handicaps, for through them I have found myself, my work, and my God."

It's challenging for us to remember that John Milton also was blind. Ludwig van Beethoven was deaf. Both Lord Byron and Sir Walter Scott were lame. But note what Byron said to Scott. "Ah, Scott, I would give all my fame to have your happiness!" And I like the note about Alice James, sister of her famous brothers William and Henry. Even though she faced physical difficulties, she was a radiant person. Her biographer says, "She never accepted the horizons of her invalidism."

These courageous people force us to think about the handicaps we all have. Some of us are handicapped by negative self-images. I talked to a man the other day who was told by his junior-high-school principal that he was not athletic and would never be able to enjoy a sport. He's lived with that false image all through the years.

For others, family and cultural conditioning have become handicaps, limiting what they are willing to do with life. Others are handicapped in how to love deeply, because of painful experiences of rejection. Still others are handicapped by previous failures that keep them imprisoned with fear of further failure. Some think they are handicapped because they lack education, good breaks, or luck.

All too many of us are handicapped spiritually because of our reaction to false religion or fear of becoming like some religious people who put us down—or off. Without commitment or vision, we may have settled in our minds what the Lord is able or willing to do in our lives today. Our constricted view of what is possible paralyzes our prayers and forces us to live on the flat, horizontal level of what we can do in our own strength.

Often people in our lives can be perceived as our limiting handicap. They can be those who hold us back, negate our uniqueness, or put down our efforts to grow as persons. Or they can be people who don't share our faith and hope for God's best in our lives. Sometimes they are people we must care for in their sickness and old age. Often they are just difficult people who place a handicap weight on us.

One day at a conference I talked about overcoming our handicaps and asked each person to identify his or her particular handicap. I could hardly believe the insensitivity of a woman who brought her husband up to meet me after the meeting. "Meet my handicap!" she said brashly. Her attitude toward him, I suspect, was her greater handicap from which the Lord wanted to set her free.

The Great Physician wants to help us with our handicaps. For those who are disabled physically or mentally, He sometimes intervenes with a healing of the disability and always is ready to maximize other faculties to the fullest, sometimes way beyond what we could imagine. And for those of us with emotional or spiritual handicaps, the Lord is constantly pressing us out on an edge of new growth. He pulls the cap off our supposed limitations and forces us to grow.

Three Groups of Handicapped People

That is powerfully illustrated by what happened one day in a synagogue on the Sabbath (Mark 3:1–5; Matthew 12:9–13; and Luke 6:6–10). As Jesus entered the synagogue He found three groups of handicapped people.

In the first group there were many good people who heard Jesus gladly, but were so handicapped by their fear and reservation that they never became loyal followers. They marveled at His mighty works, but held back by their apprehension and uncertainty, they experienced no miracle of liberation. The Master's invitation to a new, courageous life was never accepted by them personally.

Then there was the large group of the lame and blind and ill, who were in the synagogue that day seeking physical healing. Wherever the Master went, His fame as healer preceded Him, and people with hurting bodies flocked to see Him and perhaps to be healed. One of that handicapped group was the man with a withered hand. The Greek of the gospel accounts actually means, "A man who had his hand withered." And the form of the verb indicates that the withering was not a congenital dis-

ease. Perhaps he had been burned or injured in an accident.
Whatever the cause, he hoped—and watched.

There was also another group of handicapped people in the
synagogue on that Sabbath day—the scribes and the Pharisees.
They were handicapped by the rules and regulations of their
demanding religion. Their annotation of the law of Moses had
been expanded to include the most precise and minute details
of application. These specific, man-made rules had become as
important as and sometimes more important than the Ten
Commandments themselves. Legalism had become the false
god of the scribes and Pharisees. They were handicapped by
straining for absolute obedience to regulations, having lost
sight of the love of God.

The scribes and the Pharisees were particularly concerned
with the absolute obedience to the Sabbath regulations that
specifically outlined what could or could not be done on the
holy day. They were enraged at Jesus' disregard for these rules.
The fires of their indignation had been stirred into flame by
Jesus' disciples going into a field of grain, plucking, and eating
it. That would be considered work on the Sabbath and was
strictly forbidden. Added to that, Jesus had healed on the Sabbath. Now the Pharisees had come to the synagogue, knowing
that there would be sick people present whom He might heal.
They were ready, waiting and watching.

Chances are that you and I would find ourselves in one of
these three categories of handicapped people. Center your
mind on your own handicap as we watch how Jesus dealt with
the man with the withered hand.

Again focus your mind's eye on the scene. Put yourself in it.
Undoubtedly Jesus was asked to speak. He probably sat cross-
legged in front of the people, who listened with rapt attention.
Off to the side, watching and waiting with disdain, were the

scribes and Pharisees, standing, ready to move the moment Jesus broke one of their rules or regulations.

I imagine, as I picture the drama, that Jesus' attention was irresistibly drawn to the man with the withered hand. I see the man seated with his hand concealed under his cloak. His protective body language called attention to what he was hiding more than if he had exposed his hand for all to see. But Jesus was also aware of the judgmental gaze of the scribes and Pharisees. Finally they brought up the subject of the man's withered hand as a ploy to trap and accuse the Master.

"Is it lawful to heal on the Sabbath?" they asked, anticipating that Jesus would probably heal the man's withered hand. Still keeping His attention on the man in need, Jesus said to them, "What man is there among you who has one sheep, and if it falls into a pit on the Sabbath, will not lay hold of it and lift it out? Of how much more value then is a man than a sheep? Therefore it is lawful to do good on the Sabbath" (Matthew 12:10–12).

Jesus did not wait for an answer from the scribes and Pharisees in response to His pointed parable underlining the value of human life above rules and regulations. Immediately, He gave some very challenging commands to the man with the withered hand. Combining the imperatives from all three of the gospel accounts, He first said, "Arise and stand here" (Luke 6:8). Then He said, "Step forward" (Mark 3:3). And finally He commanded the man, "Stretch out your hand" (Matthew 12:13).

The three commands are significant. The man had to come out of his secret hiding of his need. In order to stand up, he probably had to expose his withered hand. When Jesus told him to step forward, he came into the full view of all the people and the leaders. In this case Jesus wanted a direct, personal encounter. The first two commands prepared for the third. The man had to be conditioned to obey the possible before he could receive the third command, which he would immediately determine to be impossible.

Often the prelude to Jesus' healing miracles today in our various needs is to give us simple instructions of things to do. Faithful obedience repatterns our wills into following His instructions. He commands us to do it. That prepares us to believe Him when He tells us to dare the impossible.

And the most impossible thing the Master could have commanded the man to do was stretch out his hand. Several things began to cooperate together to make the impossible possible. First was the man's willingness to follow the preliminary instructions. Then there was the liberation of his imagination to think what it used to be like to stretch out his hand. After that were the signals from his brain to trigger the action. And at that point divine power was released in him at Jesus' command. Muscles and tendons unused for years were energized. The miracle happened. Matthew, one of Jesus' disciples who saw this miracle that day says, ". . . And he stretched it out, and it was restored as whole as the other" (Matthew 12:13).

Two Parables—One Truth

I am convinced that Jesus taught with two parables that day. He began with the one about the sheep falling into the pit on the Sabbath. The healing was an enacted parable to drive home the truth He wanted to communicate.

Why did He choose a man with a withered hand out of the many sick and troubled people who surely were in that crowd? I think it was not only because of the man's need, but because of the significant meaning of *hand* in the life and language of Israel. The Hand of the Lord was metonymical—a figure of speech that substituted the word *hand* for the providence and presence and power of the Lord.

The Psalmist prayed, "My times are in Your hand ..." (Psalms 31:15) and "Let Your hand be upon the man of Your right hand, Upon the son of man whom You made strong for Yourself" (Psalms 80:17). The same symbolic use is made of the hand in Scripture when it is referred to as the agency of responsibility and action. Solomon said, "Whatever your hand finds to do, do it with your might ..." (Ecclesiastes 9:10).

In our own time, so many of our sayings about the ability and activity of a person are expressed in terms of the hand:

- All hands on deck
- Lend a hand
- It's in my hands
- He's a hired hand
- He has a hand at basketball
- Take this off my hands

When Jesus asked the man to stretch forth his hand, He wanted to bring the man's hand and the hand of God together. In essence, He was saying, "Let the Lord take your hand. Give Him yourself and your need. He will touch you through My command."

As you may have suspected already, I want to use the word *handicapped* in this symbolic context. When your hand—you yourself—has capped what is possible for you with fearful limitations and lack of faith, you need to allow the Lord's hand to grasp your hand and release the limiting cap.

Stretch Out Your Hand!

Think of your hand as representing you and whatever handicap limits you. Look at your hand and its five fingers. Touch each finger as you visualize reaching out your withered hand to take the Lord's hand and His healing in these five important ways:

1. The first finger of your withered hand offered to the Master is to *actualize the impossibility.* That requires His guidance. So often we want His power to accomplish something He has not willed for us. But if we ask Him, He will help us picture ourselves actually doing what He wants us to attempt. When our attention is focused on that, He will give us the power to accomplish it on His timing. That requires the second finger.

2. *Acknowledge your impotence.* If what we dare to do in overcoming our handicap can be accomplished through our own resources, it's probably not big enough to require His healing and strength. The Lord delights to press us into challenges and opportunities in which we say, "I can't do it!" Then He asks, "Do you believe I can?" When we can say, "Yes," we are on the way to experiencing a miracle.

3. The third finger is *accept Christ's imperative.* Listen very carefully to His commands. As with the man in the synagogue, the Lord will begin with us where we are and strengthen our flabby wills with some exercises. Do these at all costs. They prepare us for the big command in overcoming the limitation of our handicap.

4. Our fourth finger is crucial. It is to *accept Christ's intervention.* More than that, expect it. He is Lord of all. He has people to deploy whom we would never have expected to help us. As providential ruler of life, He can arrange circumstances we could never anticipate. But most of all, as our indwelling Lord He has power to release so far beyond our human energies and intellectual capabilities that

we will have strength we didn't think possible, and our minds will entertain thoughts beyond both our IQs and our learning.

5. Finally, the fifth finger is to *acclaim His inspiration.* Remind yourself and be ready to tell others who did the miracle. Often we are tempted to say little. That creates the impression we did what was accomplished in our own strength. I am always deeply moved when I reread the account of the healing of the ten lepers. Only one returned to praise the Lord for the gift.

Stretching forth your withered hand and placing it in the Lord's hand is a moment-by-moment, continuous process. His Spirit is present. He listens for your prayer, "Take my hand, Lord." He waits to heal and bless you.

We are post-Pentecost Christians. What Joel prophesied would happen at the time when the Lord would pour out His Spirit on all flesh is ours to experience every day:

> And it shall come to pass afterward
> That I will pour out My Spirit on all flesh;
> Your sons and your daughters shall prophesy,
> Your old men shall dream dreams,
> Your young men shall see visions;
> And also on My menservants and on My maidservants
> I will pour out My Spirit in those days.
>
> Joel 2:28, 29

Note that Joel's prophecy is nonsexist, for young and old, for masters and servants. All people are offered the gift. The three aspects of the outpouring, I think, are meant to be received by all. Consider the three gifts in a little different order from the way Joel outlines them.

When the Spirit is given, we see the vision of what the Lord wants to do. Then we dream new dreams of our actual participation in the vision. After that we prophesy. That means forthtelling plus foretelling. We forthtell what the Lord has foretold us can happen. And as a part of our prophetic gift we praise the Lord to others for what He has and will continue to do.

That's exactly what happened at Pentecost. The vision Christ had given the disciples all through the three years of His ministry with them and reiterated after the resurrection and before His ascension painted a bold picture in their minds of what could happen. Then as the days of Pentecost drew near they began to dream about it coming true. And when they received the outpouring of the Spirit, they prophesied, forthtelling to the world the wondrous things He had done.

Stand up. Go to the Lord, stretch forth your hand and pray in the words of that lovely gospel song:

> Precious Lord, take my hand,
> Lead me on, help me stand;
> I am tired, I am weak, I am worn;
> Thru the storm, thru the night,
> Lead me on to the light,
> Take my hand, precious Lord, lead me home.[1]

10 Getting the Most Out of Suffering

The title of this chapter may startle you. We all want to escape suffering, not think about what we can learn through it. Our prayers are usually for the Lord to get us out of any experience of suffering, rather than help us get the most out of it.

Yet honesty compels us to grapple with the fact of suffering in life. We endure physical pain, problems, and difficulties. We pray about them, and often our prayers seem not to be answered according to our desired timing. Waiting and wondering become excruciating. We want to tell the Lord what to do and when to do it.

The idea that there may be something we are to gain out of the waiting period is alarming, and when it goes on longer than our own perception of what is best for us, it becomes abhorrent. We steel ourselves against the possibility that there are deeper lessons to be learned through what we are suffering. Our fondest hope is that the Lord will find some other means for our growth in greatness than allowing us to wait for healing or the resolution of our difficulties.

That attitude was vividly expressed by a woman who has been attending our church. I met her one Sunday morning on my way into church. The same title as I used for this chapter had been announced in the *Los Angeles Times* as my sermon title for that Sunday. The woman had read the advertisement and had been disturbed. She stopped me and exclaimed her disquiet with urgent directness.

"Lloyd, I don't like the title of this morning's message. I've come to hear what you have to say, but I'm really uncomfortable with what that title suggests. I've enjoyed your messages about Christ's healing power in the past few weeks, but I'm really troubled about what I suspect you're going to say today. How can we get anything out of suffering, except further grief and pain? I want a Lord who can extricate me from suffering, not just help me endure it. What I think you're planning to say seems to be a contradiction to the very positive things you've been saying about Christ's power to heal us, invade our problems, and free us of difficulties. I hope your message will not negate all the hope you've engendered in us."

"Not at all!" I responded. "Yet we've all faced times of waiting for the answer to our prayers. My concern today will be to share some secrets about how to maximize those times. When we give up the assumed right to instruct the Lord about the timing of His healing in our lives, we also are released to discover what He may be saying to us. Whatever the Lord gives or withholds for a time is to draw us closer to Him in a deeper communion than we've ever known before."

The look on the woman's face indicated she knew what I

meant, yet resisted the idea because of what she was experiencing in her own life. I sensed she was probably wrestling with what seemed to her to be unanswered prayer.

"Could it be," I asked, "that you're enduring some kind of suffering right now and long for an immediate answer? Are you afraid I'm going to say that the answer may not have come because there still is something further the Lord may want to help you discover in trust and dependence on Him?"

"How did you know?" the woman replied with surprise. "Sure I am, and I'm tired of waiting. I get so impatient with the Lord's timing!"

"My friend," I said empathetically, "you and I are soul mates in the 'Lord, do it yesterday' club. Sounds like we both need a greater miracle than the immediate solution to our needs. We need the Lord Himself and what He wants for us according to His plan and purpose. I'll make you a promise. If you'll be open and receptive to what I have to say in today's message, I'll be as honest as I can in sharing what the Lord does for us in the difficult waiting periods of life."

"You're on!" she said with the first flicker of a smile I'd seen on her face that morning. Then tears welled up in her eyes. She shared a physical problem she'd been suffering for some months, which she had kept from her family and friends. My messages on Christ's healing power had attracted her to the church, but she had resisted the weekly challenge to make a complete commitment of her life and her needs to the Lord.

Praying about her needs was one thing, but turning her whole life over to the Lord's control was blocked by her self-sufficiency and pride, conditioned by years of running her own life. Now, when she found a problem she could not solve by herself, she had turned to the Lord for help. When His immediate healing was not forthcoming, she had become angry and resentful.

As our conversation ended I encouraged her to consider seriously the need to surrender to the Lord her whole life as well as her physical illness and to relinquish her determination to tell Him how and when she should be healed. I reminded her that there would be an opportunity at the end of the service for her to do that. "Trust the Lord," I encouraged. "He's never early or late. His delays are not a denial but an opportunity to receive the greatest miracle He performs in us." The woman went into the sanctuary, expectantly anticipating that promise.

Valleys of Waiting

What I talked about in my sermon that morning is essentially what I want to communicate in this chapter. Life does have its mountain peaks of triumph and delight—and its valleys of impatient waiting for our prayers to be answered. I've discovered three things about those valleys. The first two are now firm convictions. The third I have to relearn constantly.

First, it has been in the valleys of waiting for answers to my prayers that I have made the greatest strides in growing in the Lord's grace.

Second, it's usually in retrospect, after the strenuous period is over, that I can look back with gratitude for what I've received of the Lord Himself. I wouldn't trade the deeper trust and confidence I experienced from the valley for a smooth and trouble-free life.

Third, I long to be able to remember what the tough times provide in my relationship with the Lord, so that when new valleys occur, my *first* reaction will be to thank and praise the Lord in advance for what is going to happen in and through me as a result of what happens to me. I really want my first thought to be, *Lord, I know You didn't send this, but You have allowed it and will use it as a part of working all things together for good. I trust You completely, Lord!*

Do you share this desire? Do you also have better hindsight than foresight? I have 20/20 hindsight. I see so well, looking back after a difficult period is resolved, a strained relationship is healed, or a time of physical suffering is past. And I have no problem seeing ahead—hypermetropically—at a distance. I have no lack of goals and vision for the future.

What I need is to be more myopic in being able to see and interpret the deeper meaning of problems close at hand, to live more fully in the present challenges, trusting that the Lord who has been so faithful in the past will guide me through the present.

The Lord's special miracle for the valleys of life is His grace. He longs to give us a more profound experience of His unqualified love. Often He chooses to wait rather than to bless us with immediate answers to our requests, so that we can depend more fully on Him and more fully experience His grace.

That's the great discovery the apostle Paul made at a particularly difficult valley in his life. What Paul tells us about what he learned gives us the secret of how to get the most out of suffering. Read 2 Corinthians 11:16 through 12:10 very carefully. In this passage we are ushered into the apostle's inner mind and heart. One of the most dynamic Christians who ever lived opens himself with vulnerability and honesty to share his suffering and his experience of the Lord's grace in response to what seemed to be a long time of unanswered prayer.

Some background is helpful. In this section of the second Corinthian epistle, Paul makes a defense of his apostleship. In the process, he accomplishes much more than that. He gives us the key to unlock the meaning of our impatient periods of waiting for the Lord's healing of our physical needs and our difficult problems.

Paul relates several levels of suffering. The first is circumstantial. In his missionary ministry, he endured physical hardships and persecution. Our simplistic desire to be exempt from trouble is cured when we read his list of the difficulties he endured. Comparing himself and what he had been through to the false teachers in Corinth and their credentials he said:

> ... In stripes above measure, in prisons more frequently, in deaths often. From the Jews five times I received forty stripes minus one. . . . Three times I was shipwrecked; a night and a day I have been in the deep; in journeys often, in perils of waters, in perils of robbers, in perils of my own countrymen, in perils of the Gentiles, in perils in the city, in perils in the wilderness, in perils in the sea, in perils among false brethren; in weariness and toil, in sleeplessness often, in hunger and thirst, in fastings often, in cold and nakedness— besides the other things, what comes upon me daily: my deep concern for all the churches. Who is weak, and I am not weak? Who is made to stumble, and I do not burn with indignation? If I must boast, I will boast in the things which concern my infirmity.
>
> 2 Corinthians 11:23–30

In all these things the apostle had experienced the sustaining power of Christ in answer to his prayers.

Then as a further evidence of his apostleship, Paul goes on to talk about a beatific vision he was given. Though he describes it as the experience of another person, he later identifies it as his own. He was given a vision of heaven, the glory of the Lord, and heard words of truth too awesome to utter. But a mysterious thing happened. The same apostle who had endured impossible circumstantial suffering was faced with the problem of pride over the exaltation of the vision he had received.

At the same time Paul suffered a physical infirmity. There has been a great deal of conjecture about what it was. Some have suggested ophthalmia, a disease of the eyes, and still others have said that it was malaria.

The fact is that we do not know for sure. What we do know is that some physical disability caused suffering in the apostle during his first missionary journey. I am thankful that he did not explicitly name the malady. That allows us to empathize through whatever physical difficulties we endure. Most of all, we can identify with the apostle's struggle with what seemed to be unanswered prayer for the Lord's healing.

Consider carefully Paul's own explanation of his twofold struggle with pride and the physical infirmity:

> And lest I should be exalted above measure by the abundance of the revelations, a thorn in the flesh was given to me, a messenger of Satan to buffet me, lest I be exalted above measure. Concerning this thing I pleaded with the Lord three times that it might depart from me.
>
> 2 Corinthians 12:7, 8

Was the thorn in Paul's flesh his pride or his infirmity? Allow me to discuss both possibilities and then draw a personal conclusion.

A strong argument can be made that the thorn in the flesh was whatever illness Paul had suffered. If so, the apostle is saying that to keep him from inordinate pride, he was given a sickness by Satan. That sickness finally brought him to ask for the Lord's healing. Note that he suggests it was a messenger of

Satan that buffeted him with the sickness. Why? So that he would not be "... exalted above measure by the abundance of the revelations. ..."

Now consider another possible interpretation. Paul was a Hebrew thoroughly versed in the Scriptures. The term "thorn in the flesh" used in several places in the Old Testament never refers to a physical illness, but to the danger and harassment of enemies. In Numbers 33:55, Moses refers metaphorically to the inhabitants of Canaan as "... irritants in your eyes and thorns in your sides, and they shall harass you in the land where you dwell." Also Joshua describes the enemy in Canaan as "... snares and traps to you, and scourges on your sides and thorns in your eyes . . ." (Joshua 23:13). Further in 2 Samuel 23:6 David refers to the "sons of rebellion" as thorns.

Based on these references in which the metaphor of the thorn in the flesh is used only for external, human enemies, some biblical interpreters have suggested that Paul's thorn in the flesh was not his illness but the leaders of Israel who harassed him and persecuted him wherever he went. These, some reason, were the messengers of Satan sent to disturb and distress the apostle.

The deeper question concerns the methods of Satan. Would Satan want to buffet Paul to keep him from being too highly exalted in pride over his beatific vision? Hardly, since pride is Satan's most powerful tool in rendering us ineffective. That suggests a strong case for pride itself being Paul's thorn in the flesh. He had taken great pride in his sufferings at the hands of his enemies. That, plus his vision, put him in a dangerous state spiritually.

That drove the apostle to prayer. "Concerning this *thing* I pleaded with the Lord three times that it might depart from me. And He said to me, 'My grace is sufficient for you, for My strength is made perfect in weakness. . . .'" (2 Corinthians

12:8, 9, *italics added*). The words *three times* are a Hebraism for "repeatedly, frequently, persistently."

The Lord's response that His grace was sufficient has been used as a justification for unanswered prayer for physical needs or even for the impropriety of praying about our illnesses at all. It is also frequently used as a justification of the idea that the Lord does not answer some of our prayers about other needs in our lives. When someone endures a long period of waiting, we say, "Don't be so discouraged. Look at the apostle Paul. He prayed and he didn't get his prayers answered!"

On the contrary, I believe the Lord answered Paul's prayer with a twofold healing. The answer was His grace. Paul did not have to take pride in his human accomplishments or his vision to establish the authenticity of his apostleship. Christ alone was to be his sufficiency. The Greek word for "sufficient" is *arkeō,* "to ward off danger, to protect." Most important, Christ's grace in Paul's life would be perfected in his weaknesses. Here the Greek word for "is perfected" is the present passive indicative of *teleō,* "to finish, to accomplish a purpose or end."

Out of Paul's realization of his own insufficiency, he was opened to receive the sufficiency of grace. Grace is what Christ is. Unmerited, unchanging, unqualified, and unmotivated love. No merit in the apostle earned that grace. His admission of his weakness made him capable of receiving.

When the Lord said, "My grace is sufficient for you, for My strength is made perfect in weakness," He directly answered Paul's prayer. He met his deepest need. Christ's grace alone was all the apostle needed. The pride that had become a false security, standing in the way of deep communion with the Lord, had also, I think, made it difficult for him to receive the healing of his physical illness. When Paul realized anew that Christ's grace was the only basis of his status as a forgiven sinner, he could claim the healing of his body as he had so often claimed healing for others.

Paul's response to the Lord's gift of grace also must be carefully studied so we don't fall into another trap of justifying sickness or lack of answers to our prayers about any of our needs. He said, ". . . Therefore most gladly I will rather boast in my infirmities, that the power of Christ may rest upon me" (2 Corinthians. 12:9).

Does this mean that from that time on Paul delighted in being sick so that he could have the power of Christ rest upon him? I don't think so. The same Greek word, *astheneia* is translated in two different ways in this passage. Note that the translators render it "weakness" when Christ says, ". . . My strength is made perfect in weakness [*astheneia*]" and as "infirmities" when Paul says, "Therefore most gladly I will rather boast in my infirmities [*astheneiais,* dative plural of *astheneia*]. . . ." The alternative use is confusing. I suggest that "weakness" should be used in both. Nowhere else does Paul take delight in being sick. His battle with pride had brought him to his knees. He asked that it be removed, and the Lord gave him the remedial answer that had residual impact all through the rest of his life. The Lord Himself and His constant supply of grace would be all that the apostle needed.

All this discussion of the true nature of Paul's "thorn in the flesh" becomes very crucial for our growing understanding and experience of the healing ministry of the Great Physician today. It does not mean that we have a biblical basis for unanswered prayer. Just the opposite. Paul provides us with a further example that the Lord does answer our prayers for the healing of our manifold needs in all areas of our lives.

The salient thing Paul teaches us is that the confession of our weaknesses is a prelude to receiving healing power. Pride in its very subtle forms lurks at the center of our unwillingness to trust Christ with our needs. His grace is the only antidote to that spiritual sickness. Pride will prompt us to pray with a double mind. We can want solutions, answers, and healing without really wanting the Lord. And whatever it takes to break the bind of our pride—even the delay that seems to be unanswered prayer—will be used by the Lord to bring us to the place where we want Him even more than healing. Until that point of surrender, we block what the Lord wants to give us.

The Lord's Grace: Answer for Our Deepest Need

The woman I described at the beginning of this chapter discovered that the Lord understood her deepest needs. During that Sunday service after our conversation, she was given the gift of realizing that she needed the Lord's grace more than the healing of her body. At the end of the service, she did come forward, not just for prayer of healing of her physical needs, but to confess her deeper need for Christ's grace—love, forgiveness, reconciliation, and indwelling power.

During the week after that Sunday, she came to see me. She told me about the peace and joy she felt and explained, "I'm thankful that this physical problem brought me to the end of my own strength and endurance. But I discovered I was a lot sicker spiritually than I was physically. And you know, I'm not worried about the physical problem anymore. It's in the Lord's hands."

I was delighted as she gave me a progress report each week afterward when she greeted me after the worship service. She is amazed, and her doctors are astonished, at the rapid healing taking place in her body. A miracle of grace—first in her soul and now in her body. She is getting the most out of the suffering because she finally surrendered to the Lord and received not only physical healing, but an abundant and eternal life of grace.

"That's fine for this woman," you may be tempted to say. "She needed that experience of suffering to bring her to Christ. What about those of us who have been Christians for years? Must we go through struggles to keep us close to the Lord?" That question is asked me so often wherever I go.

Really it's the wrong question, asked in the wrong way. No, the Lord doesn't make life a struggle for us to keep us open to His grace. Rather, we struggle whenever we fall back on placing our confidence in anything or anyone other than His grace. Then when we realize we are in trouble, we cry out for His help. What seems to be a long waiting period of what we call unanswered prayer is really the amount of time it takes for us to realize our need of His grace as our only sufficiency. I'm constantly asked to pray with or for people who are not ready for the answer for which they want me to pray. If they received the answer before the breaking of their pride, the answer would be one more trophy of spiritual self-sufficiency.

The Lord wants us to be totally centered in Him, completely dependent on His grace alone, and unreservedly open to the flow of His Spirit within us. When we become self-sufficient with Him as an addendum to our self-willed control of our affairs, we will be thrown by the difficulties that cause suffering in our lives. Problems will engulf us and scuttle our otherwise smooth-sailing ship. Then we are forced to really pray. But when self-sufficiency has a hold on us, our cries for the Lord are contradicted by our reluctance to let go completely. Like Paul we need a twofold healing for our pride and the need that finally expresses how far from living by grace we may have drifted.

The difficulties we pass through either make us or break us.

They can make us into more receptive, Christ-centered people, dependent on His grace. If not, they will break us. The waiting time of what seems to be unanswered prayer is to make us ready for what the Lord has ready for us.

God's Greater Purpose

The deeper question is not just how we can get the most out of the difficult times we pass through, but how the Lord can accomplish His greater purpose through all that happens to us. Throughout the Scriptures there is a name of the Lord that identifies the depth of His love for us. Malachi says,

> . . . He is like a refiner's fire
> And like fuller's soap.
> He will sit as a refiner and a purifier of silver;
> He will purify the sons of Levi,
> And purge them as gold and silver
> That they may offer to the Lord
> An offering in righteousness.
>
> Malachi 3:2, 3

The picture that forms in our minds is of a refiner who has heated up the ovens, placed in the crucible the raw material from the earth, containing the precious gold or silver, and then sits watching carefully as the dross rises to the surface. The refiner skims off the dross until what remains is the pure silver or gold. He knows by experience just how hot the refining fires must be and when the purifying process is completed. When the refiner can see his own image in the molten metal in the crucible, he knows the process is complete.

When applied to our growth in greatness, the metaphors become vivid. The purpose of the Eternal Refiner is that we offer

to Him our "offering in righteousness." That's the gold mixed
in with the earth, stone and stubble of the raw material of our
humanity. Only the refining fire brings the dross of the im-
purities to the surface to be eliminated.

What is the gold of righteousness? The Lord's own nature in
us. *Righteousness* is a composite word into which all the attrib-
utes of God are magnificently collected. It is what He is, in and
of Himself. Righteousness is the Lord's loving-kindness, faithfulness, goodness, and truth. The word also describes what He
wants us to become and what is the essence of the relationship
He desires with us. He wants us to be righteous, right with
Him, reflecting His nature and doing His will. Unrighteousness
is not just doing wrong things; it's missing the reflected glory
we were meant to radiate.

That's why Christ came in the incarnation. Not only to reveal what the gold looks like, but to go to the cross to provide
us with the atonement that makes us right with God. Through
the cross we have been declared the righteousness of God.
When we accept our status as the Lord's beloved, made righteous because of what He has done for us, we are like the gold
mixed in the raw material. The refining process is not to put
the gold into us, but to take anything but the gold out of us.

Put another way, when we commit our lives to the Lord, He
comes to live in us. At first, His presence in our characters or
personalities is almost imperceptible. With our minds, we
think the liberating thought that He is *our* Lord and Savior.
But all our thinking must be captured until all thought is under
His control and an expression of His truth.

As we have considered, memories must be healed, purposes
redefined, and attitudes transformed. Our emotions must become channels of the Lord's Spirit. Our wills, previously in
bondage to self-centeredness, must be released to implement
the new direction of our thoughts and desires to glorify, love,

and serve the Lord in all things. Our relationships must become opportunities to become to others what the Lord has been to us. Selfishness, however subtly expressed in using people, must be transformed into sacrificial love, seeking the ultimate good in and for others, regardless of what it costs us.

The Refiner's Goal

In short, we were meant to be re-created in the image of Christ. That's the Refiner's goal and purpose. Paul told the Colossians that it was Christ in us who is the hope of glory (Colossians 1:27). Or worded differently, Christ in us is the glory of the gold. The refining process is to remove anything in our thinking, attitudes, or personalities that keeps the gold of His indwelling from shining with luster and beauty.

Now we are faced with another challenging question. Would it be love to leave us as excavated raw material, containing the gold, without the purifying fires that bring out the dross? Hardly. No work of the Lord reveals His love more vividly than His unlimited love expressed in His efforts to purify us. He takes us as we are, a part of His fallen creation, places His gold of righteousness in us, and then allows us to go through the fires of difficulty—not to make life a trying endurance contest, but so that we will be purged of anything that keeps the gold from its lustrous potential. The difficult things through which we pass can be accepted with joy if we believe that the Refiner is in control, separating the dross from our lives.

In that conviction is the secret of endurance in life's trials. The Lord's grace is sufficient, that is, it will accomplish its purpose. We wonder what the apostle Paul would have been like without the external, internal, and physical trials he went through. The man he was when conscripted by the Lord on the Damascus road is not the man we see emerge from the long process of refining in the quiet years of preparation in Tarsus or in the difficulties he faced all through his missionary journeys. Could the Lord have done it differently, instantly? Surely. In a moment He could have transformed Saul of Tarsus into a perfect image of Himself. Instead, He chose to do it by degrees, involving the apostle in the sublime process, allowing him to work out in all dimensions of life what He was doing in the mind and heart of the man (Philippians 2:12–16).

Or think of it in another perspective. The Lord could have left Paul the way he was. After his conversion, Paul was a recipient of eternal life. The gold of righteousness was implanted in the apostle. What if the Lord had decided not to use him as one of the most strategic personalities in the expansion of the church? What if he retired him to a contemplative life, without any challenges, trials, or difficulties? The apostle would have lived forever through Christ's election, but thousands in his lifetime and millions since would not have beheld the radiance of the refined gold of a man in Christ.

The same question becomes very personal for you and me. Would we have wanted to remain the same persons we were when we became Christians? Would we have wanted to avoid all the heat of the furnace of life that has refined the implanted gold? I wouldn't! Looking back, remembering what I've learned, how I've grown in those difficult times, and how my character has been refined, I say, "Lord, thank You for separating so much of the dross of my carnality, my willfulness and pride, and thank You for using all that's happened for Your plan and purpose for me."

The loving Refiner sits by, carefully watching, monitoring, controlling the refining process. Each day He looks at the gold of His imparted righteousness as more and more of the dross is removed. He can see Himself reflected in us, and so can others.

The apostle Peter also knew the refining fire. Across the

pages of the gospels, Acts, and finally in his epistles we see the transformation of a willful, inept, and impetuous man with immense potential changed into the image of his Master. Late in his life, Peter shared his secret of endurance with the early church. Speaking of the gift of salvation, he said:

> In this you greatly rejoice, though now for a little while, if need be, you have been grieved by various trials, that the genuineness of your faith, being much more precious than gold that perishes, though it is tested by fire, may be found to praise, honor, and glory at the revelation of Jesus Christ, whom having not seen you love. Though now you do not see Him, yet believing, you rejoice with joy inexpressible and full of glory, receiving the end of your faith—the salvation of your souls.
>
> 1 Peter 1:6–9

Note the words "if need be," referring to the grief of various trials. The words put our difficulties into a whole new perspective. Only the Lord knows what we need, when we need it, and how we need it. He doesn't send adversity. He doesn't have to—there's enough to go around in this fallen world. But how much He allows us to endure, and for how long, is perfectly balanced and timed for His refining purposes.

So let's dare to claim the refining of our gold. Recap with me the blessings that come as a result of it:

1. We are refined into the character of Christ.
2. We learn to trust the Lord and not our own plans and become recipients of His strength and courage.
3. We become empathetically sensitive to others who endure difficulties.

4. Our faith has the ring of reality, the authenticity of truth lived out in a real world.

5. We are able to radiate the true joy of Christ with courage and strength.

6. We are prepared for the quality of perfection which we will realize in full completeness in heaven.

In this light we are ready to look at Paul's response to Christ's word of grace. After he was told that the Lord's grace alone was sufficient for him, Paul made this astounding statement:

> ... Therefore most gladly I will rather boast in my
> infirmities, that the power of Christ may rest upon me.
> Therefore I take pleasure in infirmities, in reproaches,
> in needs, in persecutions, in distresses, for Christ's
> sake. For when I am weak, then I am strong.
> 2 Corinthians 12:9, 10

The apostle, now free of boasting about his visions or piety, boasts in the very things that make possible a deeper experience of the Lord's grace. His perception of the negative has been changed. The difficulties within him or without in people and circumstances have become the launching pad for greater soaring to spiritual heights. What he didn't like in what occurred around and to him became the vehicle of receiving what he wanted most of all—more of the grace of the Lord. Each emergency gave him fresh access to divine energy, each problem a renewed inflow of power.

Once again Paul is boasting. This time, however, he boasted in his infirmities or weaknesses. His beatific vision is not the source of pride any longer. Now the same energy spent in the false security of having had all the experiences given the other apostles, plus his vision, was nothing in comparison to knowing the sufficiency of grace. Then he could say that he could take pleasure in his weaknesses and difficulties. The word in Greek is *eudokeō*, "to take pleasure or to be willing." Paul was both pleased and willing to go through what he faced because it brought him into deeper communion with the Lord's grace.

Earthly Cares—God's Chariots

Hannah Whitall Smith calls earthly cares God's chariots that take the soul to its high places of trust. She based her metaphor on the story that tells of Elisha being attacked by the chariots of the king of Syria.

The prophet's servant was filled with panic at the sight of the emerging chariots and cried out, "Alas, my master! What shall we do?" Elisha was confident in the Lord's power and chariots of a far greater kind and said confidently, "Do not fear for those who are with us are more than those who are with them." And then he prayed that his servant's eyes would be opened. When the Lord responded to the prophet's prayer, the servant saw that the mountain was full of horses and chariots of fire all around Elisha.

Hannah Whitall Smith applies this to our perplexities in a very helpful way:

This is the prayer we need to pray for ourselves and for one another, "Lord open our eyes that we may see"; for all the world around us, as well as around the Prophet, is full of God's horses and chariots, waiting to carry us to places of glorious victory. And when our eyes are thus opened, we shall see in all the events of life, whether great or small, whether joyful or sad, a "chariot" for our souls."[1]

I reread that the other day when I had just received some very disappointing news. It lifted my spirits and turned my thoughts to what the Lord would do through the disappointment to show me a new phase of His strategy for my life. Then I could say, "Thank You, Lord, for this chariot to carry me on to what You have planned." Suddenly the dull ache was gone and new excitement for what the Lord had ahead filled my heart.

To take "pleasure" in life's difficulties really means to praise the Lord for them. As I said earlier, that is the ultimate level of relinquishment. We don't fully let go of our grip on things until we can praise the Lord for what has happened and what He will do to help us grow in grace through them.

Now what does all this mean as we seek to answer the central question of this book, "Why not experience Christ's wholeness, healing, and health?" A great deal. Paul's experience of what seemed to be unanswered prayer is not that at all. Nor is the account of his receiving grace instead of the healing of his thorn in the flesh a biblical justification for why the Lord doesn't heal us today. Further it is not a basis of neglecting to pray with confidence for healing. What it does teach us, however, is that a delay is not a denial.

In Paul's case, and so often in yours and mine, the Lord's timing is to bring us to something far greater than the healing of our bodies or the resolution of some difficulty. He wants to heal our pride and willfulness. Often when we seek His grace more than the healing, we become open to receiving the healing as well.

Did the apostle receive a physical healing of his physical infirmity from which he suffered in Galatia? My own opinion is yes. I base that on the fact that Luke the physician, who became Paul's companion, does not mention any continuing physical disability. His attention to detail and his honest biographical sketches of Paul would surely have included that insight from his physician's careful eye.

Perhaps it's just as well we do not know. It keeps us from simplistic theories of healing. We can't put the Lord on our agenda and demand He deal with everyone in the same way. We cannot say He will always heal with a physical remedy or that He is never concerned about our physical difficulties.

One thing *is* for sure: What happens to us on a physical or circumstantial level will be used to refine His gold in us. With that assurance we can praise Him for His grace and trust Him with the future. And that's what it means to get the most out of suffering.

3.16.85

11 The Ultimate Wholeness

I can vividly remember the angry look on the man's face. It was in stark contrast to the other joyous faces of people standing in line to greet me following a triumphant Easter service. The closer he got to me, the more I felt his hostility. Then we were face-to-face.

The man took hold of my robe and blurted out, "You have no right to ask, and I have no obligation to answer! Don't challenge us with your rhetoric about where we're going to spend eternity. We came to celebrate Christ's resurrection!"

Stunned, I wondered if the man was joking or was a mentally deranged person. His proper, well-groomed appearance contradicted the later supposition. He went on more calmly, but with equal intensity, to explain why he was so upset. In my Easter message I'd asked a question that had touched a raw

181

nerve in him. To drive home the personal reality of the resurrection as the basis of our hope now and forever, I had asked, "How many of you are assured that if you were to die today, you'd live forever with the Lord?" I had gone on to affirm that heaven begins when we meet Christ personally, accept His love and forgiveness through the cross, and receive His indwelling Spirit in our minds and hearts. Then I declared that for those who abide in Christ and He in them, death is only a transition in our eternal life.

I suspected that the question about where the man would spend eternity had upset him because he was unsure. With hundreds of people waiting behind him, I knew there was nothing to do but to ask him to wait until after I had finished greeting everyone and then to meet me in my office for a talk. He agreed.

The man I met in my office a short time later was very different from the man who had confronted me on the church steps. He started to cry as he apologized for his behavior after the service. Then he explained that a few weeks before he had been told by his doctors that he had only a short time to live. The news had thrown him into panic and had forced him to realize how unprepared he was for his own death. My direct question had exposed further how uneasy he felt. Though he'd been a Christian since boyhood, his busy life had precluded any active development of his faith or any fellowship with the Lord in prayer.

After the man had finished his apologetic explanation for his outburst, we talked at length about eternal life through Christ and how he could be sure that day that he would spend eternity in heaven. I carefully explained the plan of salvation and asked the man if he was ready to accept Christ as his Lord and Savior and know eternal security. He said he was. My Easter celebration was maximized by the joy of seeing the man raised with Christ to the new life in Him. We knelt for prayer. After his prayer of faith in Christ, he rose from his knees a different man. His face was radiant with joy.

Just before he left my office, he turned and said with a smile, "I just thought of the absurd thing I said to you after church—that you had no right to challenge me about where I would spend eternity, that I had come to celebrate Christ's resurrection. The two go together, don't they? Christ's resurrection so long ago, and now my own. Joyous Easter to you!"

A year later the man died. In the interim we became good friends. When he did pass through the valley of the shadow of death, he went calmly knowing that the Good Shepherd had him by the hand. He knew ultimate wholeness.

Our Fear of Death

I have told this man's story because I think it exposes the spiritual condition of so many people today—inside and outside the church. Our fear of death lurks beneath the surface as the source and cause of our lesser fears. Even after years of believing in Christ, we feel insecure about eternity. Death is our archenemy, feared with panic.

Whenever we take seriously Christ's healing power, we are confronted with questions about death. A woman put it flatly. "Lloyd, when we pray for a person and he dies, does that mean we've failed?"

That same question was worded with greater intensity by a friend who had just buried his wife's body. "I guess our prayers for healing didn't work. We asked the Lord to heal June, and she died."

These questions tumble about in our minds, not only after the death of a loved one, but during a serious illness when the prognosis is grim. The other day I met a member of my congregation in a shopping center. "Oh, I'm so glad we met today," she said. "I just received a call that my mother died. She was elderly, but something is haunting me. I feel terrible that I never talked to her about her eternal life. She was one of those closed people who never talked about what she believed. When she became ill a few months ago, I faced a dilemma. I didn't want to raise the question about death, because I was afraid she would think I'd given up hope of her getting well. And now, this morning, she's dead. How can I be sure about where she is?"

We're all familiar with the question that woman was grappling with in her grief. Should she have talked about death with her mother? Was there a way she could have lovingly opened the subject without its crushing her mother's hope of getting well?

I think so. Deep intimacy comes between people who dare to talk about the things both know are on each other's hearts. Some of the most profound conversations I've had over the years of caring for people have been on the subject of our death and our hope for eternal life.

Healing for Our Fears

A vital part of the healing ministry is helping people face the fact of death and receive the healing of their fears. So many Christian people have never thought and felt through their dying. I'm convinced we can't really live the on-earth years of our eternal life until our fear of death is healed. The value of a life is not calculated by its quantity of years, but the quality of its assurance of eternal life.

We're all going to live forever. The questions are where, with whom, and in what condition. A liberated Christian is one for whom heaven has begun by faith in and an intimate relationship with the Savior.

What do you think was the greatest miracle Christ performed during His earthly ministry? Our minds immediately rush to some we've considered in this book. Yet there was a greater healing than all these and the many others related by the gospel writers. One miracle the Lord performed included all the aspects of ultimate wholeness. All the other healings Jesus did provided spiritual, psychological, and physical healing. Only one person before the completed work of Calvary and the resurrection received the full measure of the salvation and wholeness Christ came to impart.

The healing ministry of Christ during the incarnation was sublimely climaxed in the healing of a very frightened, dying man. Tradition has called the man Dismas. The Scriptures do not give us his name. He was one of two men who were crucified with Jesus on Calvary. Luke describes them with the Greek word *kakourgoi,* "criminals." Careful reflection, however, suggests that they were probably revolutionaries, insurrectionists working clandestinely for the overthrow of Rome. It is unlikely that petty criminals would have been crucified for their crimes. I suspect he was a part of an underground movement against Rome and probably knew Barabbas and Judas Iscariot, both of whom, I think, were insurrectionists who were part of a band of political rebels.

We wonder if Dismas had known Jesus before that fateful day of crucifixion. Had he heard Him? Could he have been a secret follower who saw in Jesus a potential military Messiah to lead the overthrow of the mighty power of Rome? I am convinced that those were Judas's ambitions for the Master and the reason he tried to force His hand with the betrayal and arrest.

The Ultimate Healing

What we do know with assurance is that Dismas received an ultimate healing. Luke describes what happened with careful attention to the moving drama (Luke 23:39–43). When the other "criminal" picked up the jeering, scoffing jibes of the soldiers and the rulers of Israel, about the Master's claim to be the Christ, he mockingly cried out, "If You are the Christ, save Yourself and us." Dismas's rebuke to him revealed a great deal about his growing understanding of who it was being crucified next to him. "Do you not even fear God," he said to his fellow insurrectionist, "seeing you are under the same condemnation? And we indeed justly, for we receive the due reward for our deeds; but this Man has done nothing wrong." Then Dismas said to Jesus, "Lord, remember me when You come into Your kingdom." Jesus' healing word, greater than He spoke to anyone else during His ministry was, "Assuredly, I say to you, today you will be with Me in Paradise." That assurance was given to no other person until after the cross and the resurrection.

While Jesus was dying that we all might live forever, Dismas was given the gift of faith to comprehend what was taking place there on Calvary. His statement to Jesus reveals that he had heard about Christ's kingdom. He also must have heard about His claim that He would rise from the dead. Why else would he have asserted his desire to be remembered when Jesus would come in His kingly power?

I believe that it was as Dismas watched Jesus suffer on His cross that he felt and saw the authenticity of the Master's claim. Even if the only thing he knew about Jesus had been gleaned from the mocking of the crucifiers and the leaders of Israel that day, Dismas's statement to the Lord was momentous. His own plight, plus what he witnessed on the radiant face of Jesus, sealed his conviction. His confession of trust and confidence in the Lord exceeded that of all the disciples and loyal followers of Jesus. It was God's personal validation of His Son's sacrifice. Dismas was the first to receive the power of faith motivated by Jesus' sacrifice.

Jesus' response to the dying man confirms our theory. When He said "Today, you will be with Me in Paradise," He spoke with the authority of the Savior of the world. "Paradise" was the Hebrew word used to describe the realm of departed spirits. When used by Jesus in this instance, it carried the full meaning of His teaching about eternal life and heaven. Dismas would live forever in the joyous company of heaven in fellowship with Him.

The account of Dismas's salvation thunders powerful, healing truth to us. Our scoffing over deathbed conversions suddenly becomes strangely dumb. All our ideas that we can qualify for heaven by our goodness and religious achievement are swept aside. Dismas had no long list of good deeds to help him pass an entrance exam for eternal life. All he had was given him by the Spirit of God, to grasp that Jesus was indeed the Messiah, that He would conquer death, and that He had the authority to admit him to fellowship in His kingly power. He made no self-justifying claims about his record or about the refinement of his theological perceptions. Two words, "Remember me," expressed his newly found faith. And Jesus promised not only to remember Dismas, but to share the glories of heaven with him.

Think of how much more we have to base our confidence on than Dismas. We live on this side of Calvary, the open tomb, Pentecost, and centuries of the revelation of Christ's healing ministry. Ours is the developed understanding of the atonement in the epistles of Peter, James, John, and Paul. Our hope for life to the fullest now and forever is explained by their inspired pens. We have the record of how great men and women of the ages have lived with confidence and died with assurance. And the witness of the saints of the centuries is that when fear of death is behind us, our living takes on courage, gusto, and luster. We are called to live in two realms at the same time—with the perspective of heaven and with the pressures of the world. Contemplation of heaven makes a heaven out of the brief years we have here on earth.

Another time Christ promised Paradise is filled with rich and liberating metaphors. When He appeared as resurrected Lord to John on Patmos, He had an awesome promise for the troubled church at Ephesus. "He who has an ear, let him hear what the Spirit says to the churches. To him who overcomes I will give to eat from the tree of life, which is in the midst of the Paradise of God" (Revelation 2:7). Couple that with Revelation 22:2, and the picture grows more impelling.

The vision given to John of the tree of life is of a tree that bore twelve fruits, yielding them each month. The tree of life reminds us of the tree in the Garden of Eden, with the forbidden fruit of the tree of knowledge of good and evil. Now, through the sacrifice of Calvary and the reconciliation of humankind to God, the promise of eternal life is intimate communion with Him, in which we will not only know His mind and see the triumph of His plan and purpose, but will enjoy the twelvefold fruit of beatific beneficence.

Without stretching the metaphor beyond its intended purpose, I like to think of twelve fruits of eternal life in heaven. Taste some of them to whet your appetite of expectation. We will see the Lord, know Him as He is, and be known as cherished, loved members of His eternal family. We will experience constant praise as our heavenly vocation. All the finest virtues of life as we've known it will be multiplied beyond our capacity to imagine. Love, joy, peace, hope will abound in unlimited degrees. We will be given a vision of the completion of history, share in the cheering of Christ's Second Coming and welcome the elect into heaven.

In heaven we will enjoy blessed fellowship with not only our loved ones who have gone on before us, but delight in endless conversation with our heroes of the Bible and centuries since the birth of the church. We will be engaged in a ministry of intercessory influence in the lives of those we left behind at the time of our physical death. There will be no more grief or pain for us. The limits of time, physical energy, and partial knowledge will be replaced with unbounded excellence and sublimity. We will be completely whole as our earthly existence never totally freed us to be.

Assurance of Heaven

Sounds wonderful, doesn't it? Then why do we clutch on to this life so fearfully? Again, as with all the aspects of wholeness we've talked about, the assurance of heaven is inseparable from companionship with the Great Physician of our souls. The more we yield ourselves to Him, the more sure we are of our eternal destiny.

The death and resurrection of Christ are recapitulated in us now. When we surrender our lives to Him, we die to our own self-sovereignty. He raises up a new person in us, makes us whole in mind, body, and spirit. When that has been accomplished through His grace and the gift of faith He gives us, we become citizens of heaven. All physical death can do to us is release us to a fuller realization of heaven we have begun to experience now.

The last time I talked with my mother before she slipped into a coma, she said, "May I go now? I'm expected beyond. I'm ready, and I'm filled with expectation." And indeed she was. The years of knowing and loving the Savior had healed her fear of death years before. She was anxious to go to be with my dad and all the company of heaven. Often through the days of the coma and then when she left behind a tired, aged body, Paul's words kept lilting through my mind. "So when this corruptible has put on incorruption, and this mortal has put on immortality, then shall be brought to pass the saying that is written: 'Death is swallowed up in victory'" (1 Corinthians 15:54).

And what about you and me? The Great Physician longs to heal our needs during the years of this life and heal our worry about death. I remember a statement my wife, Mary Jane, made when she was going through cancer treatment. "Lloyd," she said after the Great Physician touched her body with healing power, "In the darkest hours I never had the slightest fear of death. My only concern was all of you I'd leave behind and whether my task here was completed."

I am convinced that her freedom from fear of death made it possible for her to receive healing for many more years of life in this stage of her eternal life. I couldn't help asking myself, *Lloyd, do you have that confidence?* With joy, everything within me responded, *Yes, a million times, yes! Praise the Great Physician!*

We began this book with a question. Why not experience Christ's wholeness, healing and health? And now in the focus of this concluding chapter, we ask:

> Why not settle once and for all where you will spend eternity?
> Why not claim the ultimate wholeness that maximizes the healing of all your lesser needs?

Heaven is now!

Notes

Chapter 1

1. *Choli* is rendered "sickness" or "pain" in Deuteronomy 7:15; 28:61; 1 Kings 17:17; 2 Kings 1:2; 8:8; 2 Chronicles 16:12; 21:15; and *makob* as "pain" in Job 14:22 and 33:19.

Chapter 7

1. For a more complete treatment of the function of the nervous system, see my book *Making Stress Work for You* (Waco, Tex.: Word Books, 1984).

Chapter 9

1. Thomas A. Dorsey, "Precious Lord, Take My Hand," *Hymns for the Family of God* (Nashville, Tenn.: Paragon Associates, 1976), p. 611.

Chapter 10

1. Hannah Whitall Smith, *The Christian's Secret of a Happy Life* (Old Tappan, N. J.: Fleming H. Revell, 1952), p. 235.